SCHOOL ASSEMBLIES NEED YOU!

School Assemblies
Need You!

*A starter-kit for Christians and churches
to assist with school assemblies*

RICHARD DYTER

MONARCH
Crowborough

First published 1997

Scripture quotations are from the:

Good News Bible published by the
Bible Societies/HarperCollins Publishers Ltd. UK.
© American Bible Society 1966, 1971, 1976, 1992.

New International Version.
Copyright © 1973, 1978, 1984 by International Bible Society.
Used by permission of Hodder & Stoughton Ltd.
All rights reserved.
NIV is a registered trademark of the International Bible Society
UK trademark no. 1448790

British Library Cataloguing Data
A catalogue record for this book is available
from the British Library.

ISBN 1 85424 359 4

Text illustrations by Tina McKee

Designed and produced by Bookprint Creative Services
P.O. Box 827, BN21 3YJ, England for
MONARCH PUBLICATIONS
Broadway House, The Broadway,
Crowborough, East Sussex, TN6 1HQ.
Printed in Great Britain.

Contents

Foreword

I wholeheartedly commend this highly readable and practical book about leading assemblies in schools. CARE commissioned it out of concern that 'collective worship' or assemblies in schools should be of the highest quality. By law 'collective worship' must be 'wholly or mainly of a broadly Christian character' and this requirement is leading to an increasing number of headteachers welcoming visitors from outside who are willing and able to offer assistance.

Some people maintain that the law is too demanding and wish to weaken it. 'Better,' they say, 'to have two good assemblies a week than five bad ones.' However there are many others who reject this approach and welcome the unique opportunity it gives to provide the necessary resources to present Christian beliefs to young people as part of their spiritual, moral, social and cultural development. Can we mobilise a team of volunteers to support schools as they seek to fulfil the demands of the 1988 Education Reform Act and benefit children in this way? That is the challenge. Ministers, youth workers, retired people, parents, business people and former teachers are among those who can help.

This book is a 'starter-kit' for just these people. It is underpinned by extensive research and satisfies the highest educational standards. It is not particularly aimed at teachers, although it will inspire many, but specifically at visitors from outside school. Whether you are already leading assemblies on a regular basis or whether this is all very new to you, *School Assemblies Need You!* will inspire and equip you.

As a preacher I found it a stimulating reminder of how to communicate most memorably to any audience, especially by following the pattern of Christ's own teaching methods.

Rev Lyndon Bowring

Acknowledgements

I owe an enormous debt of gratitude both to the Christian Institute, who supported my research work and provided office accommodation, and to CARE who commissioned this book. In particular, my thanks are due to Nicki Davies-Jones, Colin Hart and Ashley Smith of the Christian Institute; to John Burn, Chairman of the Christian Institute; and Alison Farnell and Ann Holt of CARE.

Many people have helped to look over the manuscript, and I am grateful amongst others to Martin Sweet (Spinnaker Trust), Chris Edwards and Zoë McKee. John Stephenson and Dot Lee (Scripture Union) have given helpful advice on the assembly scripts. Tina McKee provided the outstanding illustrations for Part Two.

I am also indebted to the numerous schools workers, Christian leaders and teachers who have responded to my requests for interviews or filled in one of my questionnaires. This book could not have been written without their goodwill.

Part One

1

School assemblies need me?

'Do you understand what you are reading?' Philip asked.
'How can I,' he said, 'unless someone explains it to me?'

Philip and the Ethiopian, Acts 8:30-31

Many people starting to read this – whether parents, grandparents, ministers, youth workers or whoever – may feel themselves to be outside of the daily life of schools. I am an 'outsider' myself, and have written this book particularly for others like me.

Many schools are genuinely pleased for 'outsiders' – like trustworthy Christian visitors – to come and help with their assembly programmes. This might involve giving a short talk, although that is by no means the only type of assistance that can be given.

Is this openness on the part of schools a surprise? No – the inspection guidelines of the Office for Standards in Education (OFSTED)[1] state that a school's approach to pupils' spiritual, moral, social and cultural development should be 'enriched by contact with the community the school serves'. Christian visitors can help to provide this contact. What is more, their input may bring valuable variety into a school's assembly programme. Recently I was speaking with a school chaplain who totted up that he had spoken to the same pupils 230 times over the last two years. He told me, 'One is desperate to get good outside speakers to vary the diet.'

This is all very well, but the question is: why should 'outsiders' freely give up their time to assist schools? Why get involved? To help answer this, I'd like to tell you what made me offer assistance for assemblies...

I happened to visit a nearby secondary school which had recently failed its OFSTED inspection, and therefore ranked as one of the worst comprehensives in the country. Attendance was appalling – during the OFSTED inspection week 50% of lessons had well under half the pupils there, and in a significant minority, attendance was often in single figures.[2]

Faced with such a problem, you might have thought that assemblies would drop down the priority list and be quietly forgotten. In fact the opposite was true. The new headteacher, who had been specially headhunted to turn the school around, saw them as a valuable means of building up the social fabric of the school. If they were valuable for that school, with all its problems, then surely they must be valuable for schools in other areas without the same extreme symptoms.

Valuable – but did it mean that 'school assemblies need me?' Surely someone else could take the initiative ...

What changed my mind was what happened in the assembly at that inner-city school. I sat at the back of a medium-sized hall which echoed with the morning chatter of thirteen-year-olds, still in outside coats that heavily camouflaged their school uniforms. Just before 9am the Head of Year asked for quiet, and the chatter subsided, though an undertone continued. As the Head entered, everyone stood up – this was an innovation of the 'clean-up' regime: respect had to be shown to his position.

As the Head started to talk, I was impressed with his gifts as a teacher. He spoke as if he was talking to each one of the pupils individually, congratulating most of them on their good behaviour during a recent OFSTED monitoring visit, and reprimanding the minority for poor behaviour, making it clear that they were letting the whole school down. Then he moved on to the moral part of the assembly. He read a story which encouraged self-belief and taking responsibility for your own life. It was very well read, and the morals it contained made me think. After he had finished reading, he applied the lesson to the pupils' lives, and then gave a personal anecdote of how his father had encouraged him when he was young to take responsibility for his life, and how he had set and worked for goals.

He ended like this:

'I'm going to finish my assembly with a very short period of reflection:

'Let us remember that we're in charge of our own destiny. We're ultimately responsible for our own success and our own future; our own sadness and joy.

'May we learn to accept responsibility for our own actions and inactions and also for our mistakes as well as for our success.

'May we face the question of what is right and what is wrong, and try to live according to our beliefs.

'May we not fall into the temptation of thinking that something is right just because we can get away with it.

'May we come to respect ourselves and stick to our principles, living out our lives in honesty and integrity.'

This message was what finally changed my mind about wanting to get involved with assemblies. Much of what was said was half right – but where was God? It's true that we are responsible beings, but Christians believe that it is God who is ultimately in charge – not us. It's true that we need to face the question of what is right and wrong, but Christians believe that God has already set out what is right and what is wrong. If all assemblies had messages like the one I'd just heard, then I could not see how pupils would have the opportunity to hear a 'broadly Christian' message – as intended by Parliament when the 1988 Education Reform Act stated that 'collective worship' (often loosely referred to as 'assemblies') should be 'wholly or mainly of a broadly Christian character.'

The respect that I felt for that particular Head left me even more convinced of the need for a huge effort from Christians to make the law on 'collective worship' work as intended. Admittedly, what I heard was one assembly in one school – it may or may not have been representative, and there may or may not have been particular reasons for adopting a certain line on that day. But evidence suggests that in many secondary schools, assemblies devoid of any talk of God are common – if they take place at all. OFSTED statistics reveal that 50% of state-maintained secondary schools don't comply even to some extent with the current law. This implies that they do not have daily assemblies, and where there are assemblies, the content is not 'wholly or mainly of a broadly Christian character.'

Compliance with the law: County Secondary Schools

(1993-4 figures)[3]	%	No. of schools[4]
Full compliance	17	600
Some compliance	33	1,200
Less than some compliance	50	1,800
Total:	**100%**	**3,600**

On a much more positive note, the situation is very different amongst primary schools, where 77% complied fully with the law on 'collective worship' in 1993-4.

Compliance with the law: County Primary Schools

(1993-4 figures)[5]	%	No. of schools[6]
Full compliance	77	14,400
Less than full compliance	23	4,300
Total:	**100%**	**18,700**

How can more 'broadly Christian' assemblies be provided for

young people? Excellent work is being done by many teachers in schools, but along with others I believe that more Christian visitors could be a part of the answer.

As you consider the figures in the table on page 16, you might ask as I did: 'amongst all those schools, what difference could I make as just one individual? What's the point of getting involved when there are so many schools with minimal Christian input into assemblies?'

On reflection, I don't think that those are the right questions to ask. I know that in my own case, I have the opportunity to offer assistance to schools – not everyone does. So for me – and who knows, perhaps for you – the question is really 'how am I using the resources that I have to meet the needs that are immediately around me?'

* * *

Do assemblies do any good anyway, whether 'broadly Christian' or not? I believe they are worth investing time and effort in, and I'd like to show you some of the opportunities that exist by asking you to visit two school assemblies with me in the comfort of your imagination.

Our first visit is to a comprehensive in a 1960s new town. We are going to help Alan, a regular Christian visitor to the school, with his Tuesday assembly to Years 7, 8, and 9 (eleven to fourteen year olds).

Imagine that we are standing together rather nervously at the front of a high-ceilinged hall, capable of accommodating about 500 people. Pupils are flooding through the door on our left. Some glance at us as they come in. There's no hostility, but neither is there any welcome. They are immersed in school life; this is just another session, and the school day is full of sessions. Everything is on a large scale – large hall, large number of pupils; a sense of formality.

Teachers are entering too and urging quiet, but the hall is still full of rustlings and steps and murmurs. The pupils vary enormously in size. The Head of House comes over to us; he's tall and in his late thirties. Alan introduces us, and he greets us civilly.

'It's always good to see you,' he says. 'It gives the kids

another face to look at. We like to have a bit of variety in assemblies, rather than have me banging on at them all the time'.

If you were to glance now back to the main hall, you would see that almost all the chairs are filled. It's the moment when you remember what a solid mass 450 people makes. We're only three amongst all those people, yet everyone is looking towards us, not to any of the other 447. This is the moment when I can feel my stomach sinking lower, yet also when my mind becomes clear and fixed.

The Head of House asks for quiet, and then starts to introduce us to the pupils. The few moments in which he talks seem almost like a reprieve – the assembly has started, and we haven't had to do anything yet. Then he turns to us, and we're on.

Alan's first words are loud enough so that everyone can hear, and confident enough so that they know that he's in control. 'Good morning. When I was invited to take this assembly, I was told that this week's theme is 'daring, caring and sharing'. When I heard this I started to wonder what a really good example of this would be. I'm a Christian, and I believe that an outstanding example of 'daring, caring and sharing' is... Jesus.

'I'm going to say more about why I think that in a few moments, but first I'd like to work through an illustration with you. Could I have two volunteers to help me?' A few hands go up, and Alan chooses a girl and boy from the front row. He asks them to stand on each side of the lectern from which he's speaking.

'I'm going to be giving money to my volunteers. Not real money like this, unfortunately' (he waves a ten pound note) 'but pretend money.

'The volunteer standing on the right is going to have loads and loads of pretend money. She is "Ms Rich" – look at all these notes. The volunteer on the left, on the other hand, only gets two notes. He is "Mr Poor".

'We're going to have an example of caring and sharing. Ms Rich, could you please share some of your wad of notes with some of the people in the front rows – that's right, give quite a lot away...

'Now, Mr Poor, it's your turn. I know you've only got two

notes, but could you give one of them away to somebody on the front row....

'I'd like to suggest to you that Mr Poor has actually been a better example of caring and sharing than Ms Rich. Ms Rich had loads of money to start with and still has loads of money even after giving some away; Mr Poor, on the other hand, didn't have very much, and he really notices what he's given.

'That was the first stage of our example of caring and sharing. For the second stage, my volunteers are going to have something more precious than money to give away. It's not silver or gold, but... life. Our lives are much more precious, because without it, money and possessions are worth nothing to us.'

Alan takes back the pretend money, and hands to each volunteer a card with a heart-beat scan on it representing life. He also has one for himself.

'Each of us has only one life. Consider giving this away to other people. It would be very difficult to do, much more difficult than it was for Mr Poor to give away half of what he had. I don't know about my volunteers, but I would have to think very carefully about giving away my life.' Alan asks for the volunteers' agreement to this.

'Christians believe that Jesus did give his life for other people. That's why I said earlier that Jesus is an outstanding example of daring, caring, and sharing.

'I want to say something more on this, but firstly, thank you to my volunteers – please could you sit down.

'The Christian symbol is a cross' (Alan holds up his fingers in the shape of a cross). 'That symbol reminds Christians of Jesus' death, and reminds us that when Jesus was killed on the cross he said that he was giving his life for his friends.

'It wasn't easy for Jesus to give his life. The Bible tells us that the night before he died, Jesus was praying to God and saying, Heavenly Father, if it's possible, is there a way that I don't have to go through with giving my life?

'But then he prayed, "Yet not my will, but yours be done" *Not my will, but yours be done.* Jesus did what God the Father told him, and that's how he dared to give his life...' (Alan picks up the heart-beat card) '...for other people' (Alan lays the card carefully onto the front of the lectern, and there is a slight pause while he does this).

'This raises several questions, and I want to look at just one of them during the last two minutes of this assembly. It's something that was important for me when I was thinking about Christianity. And the question is: how can I get to be like Jesus?

'Let me explain with an illustration. Here I have two glasses' (Alan holds two tall glasses in his raised hands, one full of water, the other with Ribena). 'This glass is a nice glass and we'll call him Fred. Fred the glass. Fred has got something ordinary inside him – tap-water.

'This other glass – let's call this the Jesus glass. It's got something special inside it – Ribena! Fred looks over at the Jesus glass and thinks "I want to be like that." So he starts to try and make himself like the Jesus glass. He shakes up and down, swirls round and round, does everything he can think of... but in the end, it's still just water.

'What Fred needs is help. If he asks the Jesus glass for help...' (Alan pours some of the Ribena from the 'Jesus' glass into 'Fred', gradually changing the tapwater into blackcurrant juice) '...then Fred can change.

'In some ways, Christians believe that this is a picture of us. We are naturally like Fred – we have ordinary attitudes, like "I want to do the things I want and I don't want to give too much to others – my will be done". Sometimes we try to change, but really, we can only change if we have help. Christians believe that we need to turn to Jesus and ask him for help.'

'There are two things I'd like you to remember from this morning's assembly. Firstly, Jesus is a great example of daring, caring and sharing. Secondly, Christians believe that to follow his example, we need Jesus' help.

'I'd like to encourage you to think about those things. I know that you normally have a few moments of silence after an assembly talk, so let's just be quiet for twenty seconds and think.'

Alan has already explained to us that he finds out what the school normally does about prayers or about periods of reflection, and fits in with whatever the pupils will be used to. Many secondary schools, he finds, do not normally use formal prayers. He would always try, however, to have some opportunity for reflection or private prayer as part of his assembly.

In the hall, there is a time of near-silence lasting no longer than the twenty seconds Alan promised. Then Alan says 'Thank you for listening', and our part of the assembly – the part which constitutes an 'act of collective worship' – is over. Now it is time for the administrative part of the assembly. The Head of House returns, looking slightly more harassed as he takes over the limelight of being the authority figure at whom the pupils are looking.

'I'm sure we'd like to thank our visitors for what's been said. These are important issues, and I also urge you to think about them. After assembly, I want to see those six boys that were caught smoking behind the physics block. You know who you are, and I have a list of your names. I have a message from Mrs Fitzgerald; could all of you in the stage crew for the school play attend a short meeting at 1.30 pm tomorrow in this hall. That's the stage crew, here, at 1.30 pm. Don't forget. Thank you.'

The form tutors, who have been ranged along the side of the hall, jerk into life and start dismissing pupils row by row. There is no visible reaction; none of the pupils come up to say 'well done'; most of them have the same expression as when they came in – off to another session, and the school day is full of sessions. Finish one, and then go to another.

When the hall is almost empty, the Head of House comes up to us, his supervision job done. His authority act is laid aside, and once more we see a smiling man. 'Thank you, that was great,' he says. 'I always think it's good to have visitors who can talk personally about their faith, and what it means to them.' Alan nods. It's very important for him, too, that young people can relate faith with a person who believes it. It helps break down stereotypes – Christians are real people who come into schools just like ordinary people – they are not like the media images of religious people cooped up inside a church. It's what Christian visitors are, as much as what they say, that makes a difference.

The Head of House goes on, 'You know, although we never see many immediate results from assemblies, and although we're sometimes told that they're dull and repetitive, you'd be surprised at how older pupils and leavers comment on things they've learnt from them – long after we've forgotten what we said.'

As the Head of House walks away to go to his next class, I wonder what he makes of us as Christian visitors. Possibly, he thinks we're slightly fanatical. But it's more likely that he simply accepts that we are local representatives of the Christian faith, freely giving our time, and as such a useful resource for the school.

The last thing we do is to discuss how the assembly went, and to give feedback and comments to Alan. As I did no talking, I was able to look at the faces of the pupils and see when they were interested and when they weren't. The illustrations – particularly the glass idea – worked well. For next time, perhaps the talking between the two illustrations could be a little bit sharper?

* * *

Now for our second visit. This time it's an independent girls' junior school set in the heart of a leafy suburb. We are with Bill, a full-time Christian schools worker. He's given us a lift to the school in his battered Volkswagen Polo which he parks beside a gleaming blue BMW with personalised number plate. The school is much smaller than the comprehensive, and has a more homely feel, helped by bright displays of artwork and pictures.

Bill never wants to risk letting the school down by being late, and even when we have signed in with the school secretary and sent a message to the Deputy Head to reassure her we've arrived, we still have fifteen minutes to talk amongst ourselves. We stand in the gym which doubles as an assembly hall, and Bill explains that fee-paying schools are not bound by the 1988 Act which requires 'collective worship' wholly or mainly of a broadly Christian character, but nevertheless many of them place great emphasis on daily assemblies. In this particular school, he knows that they have regular Christian assemblies, and this has influenced the content of the talk he's about to give. Since it's nearly Easter, he'll be explaining why it's a special time for Christians.

Promptly at 8.55am, the girls enter the gym following their class teacher, much like ducklings following a mother duck. They sit cross-legged on the floor except for the privileged top class who sit on a hard wooden bench at the back. The calming sounds of the Adagio from J. S. Bach's *Easter Oratorio* waft from a CD player, and the girls look expectantly towards the front.

The Deputy Head takes the lead in introducing Bill. He's here, she says, for a special Easter assembly that will make everyone think. It's quite a billing to live up to! Bill starts by reminding everyone of the last time he visited, and how much he liked listening to their singing. This time, he announces, he's going to teach them a song. He picks up his guitar, turns on his overhead projector (OHP) so that the words appear on a screen, and starts to teach them the tune and, just as importantly, the actions that go with it. The children love it. Looking at the line of teachers along the side of the gym, you would see them doing the actions too, some self-consciously (particularly some of the younger ones), others very happy to be part of the fun.

When everyone has got the hang of the song, Bill puts away his guitar and starts on his talk. He holds up two polystyrene cups connected by a piece of string and explains that this is his very own telephone. He asks for two volunteers from amongst the older girls of Year 6, and chooses two from amongst the sea of hands that shoot up. Bill demonstrates how the 'telephone' works with one of the girls.

Bill says, 'We're going to use this simple telephone to tell a Bible story. I'd like you to use your imaginations for this story.'

At the front there are three benches joined lengthways with a sign sticking up saying 'Heaven'. As pre-arranged with Bill, I stand on the bench to represent 'God'; one of the volunteers sits cross-legged beside me. The second volunteer sits directly below me about two feet forward of the bench, close to a large sign saying 'Earth' and with a smiling face drawn on it.

'In the beginning, God…' (Bill gestures towards me) '…created the heavens' (he points to the benches and the sign) 'and the earth'[7] (he points towards the sign on the floor). 'He created people[8] who live on the earth – and I'd like you to imagine that the volunteer sitting on the floor represents "people".

'To begin with, Christians believe that God and people were good friends. To show this, I'll give one end of our simple telephone to "God", and the other to the people. You can see that whenever God talks, people can easily hear – could you give a demonstration of that please? …And also, it's easy for people to talk with God.

'That was how it was to begin with. But the Bible tells us that one day people turned away from God, and didn't want to listen any more to what he said.[9] To show this, I'm going to give a pair of scissors to "people". Why don't you cut the string – then you can be sure that you won't have to be bothered by God any more.

'People no longer listened to God. Christians believe that they became enemies of God, and they also believe that God punishes his enemies.[10] Things were spoilt.'[11] Bill turns the sign 'Earth' around to show an unsmiling face.

Bill asks me to talk into my cup, and as I do this Bill holds up the loose end to show that the link between God and men was cut.

'Christians believe that God will punish his enemies.[12] This was a big problem. But Christians believe that God had a plan to save people from being punished. The Bible...' (Bill picks up and opens his Good News Bible) '...says that God loved the world so much that he gave his only Son, so that everyone who believes in him may not die but have eternal life.'[13]

Alan asks Jenny, the volunteer beside 'God' on the bench, to go down to 'Earth' and tie the two loose ends of string back together. He explains that she's a bit like Jesus, God's Son.

'That was a fairly easy thing for Jenny to do, but it wasn't as easy for Jesus to repair the link between God and man. Christians believe that nothing less than Jesus' death could change the way things were. It will soon be Easter, and one of the special days of Easter is Good Friday. Good Friday is when Christians remember that Jesus died on the cross.' Bill holds up a simple cross in his left hand. 'And Christians believe that he did this so that...' Bill holds up the knot with his other hand '...so that people could be friends with God again.[14]

'On the third day after Jesus died, Christians believe that he came back to life and went up to heaven' (the volunteer representing 'Jesus' stands on the right of 'God' on the bench). 'That's what we remember on Easter Sunday – the third day after Good Friday.

'What happened at the first Easter has made a big difference. Christians believe that now people have a choice of two things they can do. Either they can continue to ignore God and do their own thing, just like people did in the past. Christians believe that if they do that, they'll still be enemies of God, and that's a bad thing to be. Or, they can turn back to God...' (Alan takes up the cup and puts it to his ear) '...and be friends with God – because of what Jesus has done.

'When I decided to become a Christian ten years ago, that's

what I did – I turned to God and believed in Jesus, and stopped ignoring what God told me to do.'

There is a pause, then Alan says, 'I'd like to finish with a short prayer; first could my volunteers sit down on the chairs just here...

'I'm going to read a Christian prayer; if you agree with it, perhaps you could say 'Amen' at the end. 'Amen' means 'I agree'. Please could everyone close their eyes and bow their heads.

'Heavenly Father, thank you for making us.

Thank you that we can be friends with you because of Jesus.

Please help us to know you more.

Amen.

Alan concluded by saying that he would be at the Christian club at lunchtime (he had asked the Deputy Head for permission to make this 'advert' in advance). He encouraged anyone interested to come along and hear more about the Christian message of Easter.

* * *

Two examples of schools and their assemblies. If you have been imagining you visited those schools, you would have seen something of what Christian visitors can do when they take assemblies in schools. Short talks like these can make a difference – many children are currently ignorant of even the basics of Christianity. A recent survey has shown that 49% of 16-24 year-olds do not know what Good Friday commemorates.[15]

* * *

Do school assemblies need you? They may do – there is certainly a need for trustworthy Christian visitors to take the initiative and offer to serve schools. Supporting Christian assemblies may not be easy to do, but the next chapters look at ways of overcoming some common problems...

2

…But what would I say?

'Christians believe that…'

At one time I was fortunate enough to work on the advertising of one of the largest brands of household products in Britain. Hundreds of man-hours and millions of pounds were lavished on a succession of TV commercials. There is no way that so much money would have been invested unless it was believed that messages – even ones that last for less than sixty seconds – can have an impact. Now consider the fact that an assembly talk may last over ten times as long as a commercial…

The impact an assembly can have is not only an incredible opportunity, but also an incredible responsibility. St James warned us that 'not many of you should presume to be teachers, my brothers, because you know that we who teach will be judged more strictly'. If you're thinking that you might be interested in leading assemblies yourself, then the question of 'what would I say?' is crucial.

I hope that this chapter will be of value to you both if you're already experienced in taking assemblies, or if you've really not done much before. We'll be looking at three main areas:

1. Content: What to say

1. Content :
What to say

2. Structure:
When to say it

3. Presentation:

How to say it

Four things influence the content of any assemblies led by Christians visiting schools:

Legislation
Christian Truth
Sensitivity to pupils
School policy

a) The content should be consistent with relevant legislation and guidelines

Under the 1988 Education Reform Act, schools in England and Wales must provide daily acts of collective worship wholly or mainly of a broadly Christian character. 'Collective worship' is generally referred to as 'assemblies' in schools.

The Government's Circular 1/94 (which relates to collective worship and Religious Education) says:

Collective worship in schools should aim…
    …to provide the opportunity for pupils to worship God, to consider spiritual and moral issues and to explore their own beliefs;
    …to encourage participation and response, whether through active involvement in the presentation of worship or through listening to and joining in the worship offered
    …and to develop community spirit, promote a common ethos and shared values, and reinforce positive attitudes.

(Circular 1/94 Paragraph 50)

Circular 1/94 makes it clear that the 'worship' to which it refers is not expected to be the same as in a church service. Paragraph 57 states:

> ...worship in schools will necessarily be of a different character from worship amongst a group with beliefs in common.
> The legislation reflects this difference in referring to 'collective worship' rather than 'corporate worship'.

It would be fair to say that there is a considerable debate about what actually constitutes 'worship'. A senior adviser to OFSTED, addressing a meeting of the Parliamentary Christian Fellowship,[1] talked about OFSTED's thinking as follows:

> We felt that there was no magical ingredient that determined that an activity was worship, it was the focus which was important...[2]
> You might want to reflect at some stage on what you think of hymn practices... (there are) hymn practices which are deemed to be an act of worship and hymn practices which are not deemed to be acts of worship. Now I find that perfectly consistent because I have been in schools where I have come to those conclusions – where I have felt that the hymn practice was indeed an act of worship and in others where I have felt that it was not an act of worship...[3]

Circular 1/94 reiterates the 1988 Act's emphasis on 'broadly Christian'. Paragraph 61 states that collective worship should not be distinctive of any particular Christian denomination.

Circular 1/94 also contains the following guidance on making collective worship appropriate for pupils:

> The extent to which and the ways in which the broad traditions of Christian belief are to be reflected in such acts of collective worship should be appropriate to the family backgrounds of the pupils and their ages and aptitudes. It is for the head teacher to determine this after consultation with the governing body.
> Pupils who do not come from Christian families should be able to

join in the daily act of collective worship even though this would, in the main, reflect the broad traditions of Christian belief...

Circular 1/94 provides guidance applicable to schools in England and – with minor alterations – Wales. Legislation concerning Scottish schools is, however, different: details are available from the Department of Education and Employment.

b) The content should be faithful to the Christian faith

Once I asked a local minister to give his comments on a practice assembly script I had been preparing on the theme 'don't swear'. He didn't like it, and after a time I began to see why. He argued that if a person is invited as a representative of the Christian faith, it makes sense for that visitor to talk about things important to Christians. Whilst there may be nothing wrong with an 'anti-swearing assembly' in itself, a Christian visitor who never went further than 'let's just be nice to each other' would not be getting to the heart of what Jesus was about. Christianity is not only about ethics.

Following that talk with the minister, I now try to write out a 'learning objective' for each assembly. This always starts with the words 'Christians believe that...'

Below this I write down a 'Biblical basis' – verses which ground the belief in Scripture. This helps to ensure that every assembly presents a Christian truth, and if I've been invited as a Christian, I do think that this is a fair thing to do.

For example: Christians believe that faith is believing God's promises. In Romans 4:18-21 Abraham believed and hoped, even when there was no reason for hoping. His faith did not leave him, and he did not doubt God's promise. I try to base my assembly scripts on a story or sermon in the Bible as then I can be more confident that the message is genuinely Christian. Also, I can be more confident that it will be thought-provoking and have an effect, since St Paul tells us that the gospel is 'the power of God' (Romans 1:16).

At some point in an assembly I would try to include a short application of the belief that has been chosen, showing how it has a practical effect on life.

c) The content must be sensitive to the pupils to whom you're speaking.

Everything that is said in assembly needs to be tempered by a prudent consideration of the audience and environment (school not church).[4] For example, an appeal for a decision for Christ would *not* be appropriate.

Sensitivity to the background of the pupils Remember that the headteacher is supposed to have determined how to make 'collective worship' appropriate for pupils (Circular 1/94), and many schools have now developed written policies on the subject. Checking your content in advance with a senior teacher is a good way of ensuring that you are keeping the spirit as well as the letter of the policy.

Sensitivity to pupils' aptitudes and knowledge base Pupils in schools that regularly have Christian assemblies will have a different knowledge base to those where religion is hardly ever mentioned. You might feel that even some of the simple assembly outlines given later in this book assume too much background knowledge for schools you know.[5] Visiting a school's 'normal' assemblies could be one way of finding out what pupils are used to.

Sensitivity to the ages of the pupils Some basic differences between primary and secondary levels are summarised in the table overleaf:

Primary schools	Secondary schools
The illustration (eg story or piece of drama) tends to be the main part of the assembly, and an idea is then drawn out at the end	Ideas are more to the fore
Singing is common	Singing is not common
Prayer is common	Prayer is not common – pupils are more likely to be asked to 'think about what's been said'

d) The content must be acceptable to the school

Visitors are only allowed into school at the invitation of the teachers, and their rules must be followed. No visitor has a 'right' to lead an assembly – it is a privilege extended by the school.

Schools quite rightly demand good standards from visitors. The Head of Humanities in an inner-city comprehensive warns: 'Taking assemblies is a skill. Just because a person is a Christian does not mean they are able to speak meaningfully to a large group of young people. Our pupils will always behave well, but they have the right to have high expectations of the assembly. An ill-prepared speaker who has not had the appropriate experience is not doing their faith any good.'

Many schools have themes for each term or half-term, and visitors will be expected to fit in with them. One respondent to my survey of church leaders put it this way: 'I try to plug into the curriculum. For example, when the theme was "our favourite book", I talked about the Bible.'

Christian visitors do need to be professional in communicating with young people. If they do a poor job, they will not be asked back, and, perhaps worse, may cause the door to be shut to other visitors.

2. Structure: When to say it

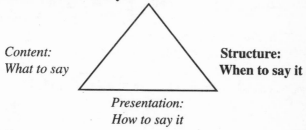

Content:
What to say

Structure:
When to say it

Presentation:
How to say it

Structure can be thought of as the route by which pupils are taken from things they know to things that they don't know. It could be visualised like this:

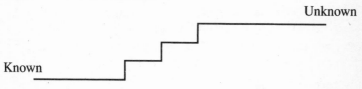

Unknown

Known

The 'staircase' cannot take longer than about ten minutes for pupils to 'climb', so there cannot be too many steps. In primary schools the steps will be fewer and simpler than for older pupils.

The following approach might be helpful if you're thinking about how to form a 'staircase' to communicate a Biblical idea:

Step 1: Find something pupils relate to
|
Step 2: Bring out the idea behind it
|
Step 3: Contrast it with the Biblical idea
which is your learning objective

This seems to me to be how Paul approached his talk at the Areopagus:[6]

Step 1: Find something people relate to
Paul started by talking about how he'd noticed that Athenians were religious, and how he'd looked carefully at their objects of worship

I

Step 2: Bring out the idea behind it
Paul pointed out that one of the altar inscriptions ('To an unknown god') showed that the Athenians didn't actually know God

I

Step 3: Contrast it with the Biblical idea which is your learning objective
Paul said that he did know God and he went on to proclaim God to them.

A practical example

As an example, opposite is the 'staircase' in Alan's secondary school assembly that was given in the last chapter.

Alan's assembly wasn't bad, but now that the structural bare bones are revealed, it could be argued that it is flawed as a piece of communication. Why is that? The mistake is to have two learning objectives. Within the short time of an assembly, trying to get two different points across is very challenging.

Here is an actual written comment from a teacher on what he thought Alan's assembly was about:

'Establish the importance of daring, sharing, and caring. Relatively easy to share if you have plenty. When a person with only limited possessions shares it is a major undertaking. Jesus as an example.'

This comment suggests that Alan's second learning objective

Alan's assembly

Learning objective:
1. Christians believe that Jesus is an outstanding example of 'daring, caring and sharing' – he gave his life for the sake of others
2. Christians believe that people need to ask for Jesus' help to follow his example

Summary of steps:
Step 1: It's hard to give to others when you don't have much yourself

Step 2: It's would be very hard to give your life to others – you only have one life

Step 3: Christians believe that Jesus did give his life for others

Step 4: In doing this, Jesus was being obedient to God's will

Step 5: Christians believe that people need to ask for Jesus' help to follow his example of love

---

'Christians believe that people need to ask for Jesus' help to follow his example' was not successfully communicated.

The way to improve Alan's assembly (which I originally wrote) would be to concentrate entirely on the first learning objective. At the moment, steps 1-4 form a staircase that goes into the unknown area of 'what did Jesus do?' As a general principle, there should be only one staircase per assembly. Step 5 could have been another step up that staircase, perhaps applying what has already been said to pupils lives (for example: 'how do we find out what God's will is?'). In fact, step 5 goes well beyond application of what has already been said – it actually switches to a related but different staircase that goes into the area of 'how can I be like Jesus?'

It might be better to save what is said in step 5 – the illustration with 'Fred the glass' and the 'Jesus glass' – for another 'one staircase' assembly. That assembly might have a structure like this:

Learning objective:
Christians believe that people need to ask for Jesus' help to follow his example

Summary of steps:
Step 1: People often think they can be good enough for God by their own effort
Step 2: However, none of us can keep God's laws completely
Step 3: Christians believe that only Jesus kept God's laws perfectly
Step 4: Christians believe that we need Jesus' help to follow his example
(show illustration with two glasses – 'Fred' and 'Jesus')

This structure could communicate the idea much more powerfully than tagging it onto the end of an assembly that is mainly about another idea. Keeping ruthlessly to one learning objective will make it less likely that your audience will miss a point you really want to get across.

Structure for a school audience

A short while ago I wrote an assembly script in which I definitely had just one learning objective, and where I had been at considerable pains to make each step follow on logically from one another. I read it out to a friend, and was rather surprised to find that he was less impressed with the smooth flow than I had been. He suggested that if pupils lost concentration at any point (not suggesting, of course, that he had done so himself) then they could miss out a step and find themselves confused, even though it would have been crystal clear if only they had listened carefully. Given human nature, why didn't I try recapping at various points, and perhaps make the same point in more than one way to consolidate it? Rather than a smooth staircase, the ideal structure might look more like this:

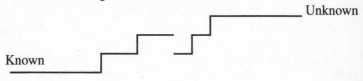

In other words:

    Tell them what you are going to tell them;

    Tell them;

    Tell them what you have just told them.

3. Presentation: How to say it

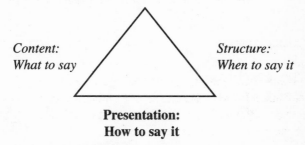

Making assemblies interesting ...

One vicar who wrote to me about assemblies was blunt about the problems of making assemblies interesting for young people. 'Clergy can fall flat on their faces. We think we know how to speak in public. But doing a ten minute talk to young children is very different from preaching to a congregation.'

He's right about the importance of making assemblies interesting to young people – but don't think that it's only worth becoming involved if you can do an all-singing, all-dancing multi-media presentation. Keeping pupils' interest is a 'means', not the 'end'. Simple things – perhaps a story – can be enough to gain their interest and so allows them to take in your message. And it's hearing your message that matters most.

In the assembly scripts in chapter 7, you'll see a number of devices that are designed to keep pupils' interest. These should not just be at the beginning to grab attention, but also at various points throughout the assembly. Having a long 'serious' section is likely to have pupils switching off. This can be very off-putting for the speaker, particularly if teachers as well as pupils start to look rather bored, and perhaps fold their arms and sigh inaudibly, or else get out a memo to read. To avoid this experience, 'serious' and 'fun' need to be integrated.

Devices to keep interest include:-

● Asking for volunteers and getting them to do an activity.
● Inviting pupils to express their opinions through a show of hands.
● Using props.
● Using visual aids like OHP slides.
● Telling a story.
● Talking about your own experience.
● Using humour.
● Using an analogy.
● Using quotes that are memorable and provocative.
● Doing a drama.
● Singing.

Some of these devices are more suited to primary than secondary pupils, and vice versa: please see table opposite.

Here are some comments on presentation from people who visit schools regularly:

I have tried different ways to make the talks interesting and relevant. Now I usually go as a 'farmer' – I still work as a farmer despite taking early retirement from lecturing – and take a sheep or dove or equivalent. The result is that the children (and most staff)

	Comments
Asking for volunteers and getting them to do an activity	It's generally easy to get volunteers in primary schools, but can be more difficult in secondary schools, especially above Year 9 Beware of using real people as 'stooges' – volunteers should have a role, and not just be left to stand about. If they have nothing to do, they first look uncomfortable, then bored, then start to whisper – distracting everybody else
Asking questions of the audience	If you're going to ask questions in general, you should be confident that you can control the response – particularly in primary schools, your question could prompt private conversations, and therefore loss of attention
Using props	Physical props work well, as you can point to them, move them around and so on – they can be more flexible than OHP slides
Using visual aids	'Bigger is better' is a general rule Remember that displaying words (for example on an OHP) does not constitute a visual aid – there need to be pictures, diagrams, etc. If you do use words, keep them to a minimum – some pupils may not read well. Use lower case lettering for primary-age pupils, as younger pupils may not be able to read words entirely written in capitals
Using humour	Don't let the flow of your assembly be affected even if nobody laughs at the things you thought would be funny

enjoy the assemblies. I have been asked to more schools and now cover all age groups. Careful and lengthy preparation is always needed to make assemblies good.

Congregation member at an Anglican church

I take assemblies from time to time, using an overhead projector to illustrate stories. This seems to work, especially in this visual age!

Church secretary of a Baptist church in Middlesex

You have to work harder to get attention if you don't have a relationship with the children. Where I know the school, I find it quite easy. In schools which I don't visit regularly, I use more, simple visual aids.

Church leader, Northumberland

Iain, a Youth for Christ schools worker, shares the concern to present the message in an interesting way. He says, 'I focus on things that children will be familiar with, like common advertising slogans. It usually sticks in their minds. It's really important to link into their culture, to communicate in an exciting and interesting way, in a way that sparks things'. One word of caution on advertising slogans – they quickly become obsolete, and it's easy to fail to connect with what pupils are watching at the moment. For example, I have attended an assembly that used the classic slogan of 'who would you give your last Rollo to?' as an introduction to the idea of sacrifice; however, this has not been used in advertising for the last few years, and I doubt that young people still recognise it.

Similarly, care needs to be taken about what news items are picked up on – young people may not have a deep background knowledge of current affairs. Nevertheless, newspaper stories can be good starting points to get pupils' attention.

Talking about personal experience People like to find out about other people. If you're standing at the front and talking about your own experience, then pupils can relate an example of behaviour to an actual person they can see. It helps to keep things concrete. As an old saying goes: 'Personal experience hits the mark where theory misses.'[7]

A full-time schools worker said, 'In some ways I'm acting as a role model when I stand up as a Christian in front of young people, so I think it's good if I can talk naturally about my family life, my relationship with my wife and children, and so on. It also helps break down barriers if I'm open with them.'

For myself, I know that some of the most vivid stories and anecdotes I've heard have been told by speakers recalling things that actually happened to them. If you think about the things you remember from talks you've heard, you might come to a similar conclusion.

Reinforce words with actions You can increase the impact of what you say by using actions to reinforce the meaning of your words as you say them. Next time you watch an advert, watch how the pictures and action exactly match the words that are being spoken – usually you will find that the 'audio-visual synchronisation' is very close.

A simple example:

Words	Action that could reinforce the meaning of the words
'This is not what it's about'	Write the idea that you're rejecting on some paper, and then scrumple it up as you say these words. Alternatively, deliberately throw away the prop that has been used to represent the rejected idea

Using analogies An analogy is where a parallel case is used to develop a line of reasoning. For example, St James writes: 'Although (ships) are so large and are driven by strong winds, they are steered by a very small rudder wherever the pilot wants to go. *Likewise* the tongue is a small part of the body, but it makes great boasts.'[8]

Analogies work well if the parallel is close. I find that all too often it isn't. In my own experience, I know that I have latched onto a good story, or an event that's amusing or odd, and think, 'yes, I'll use that'. I then spend a long time spent trying to develop the parallel line of reasoning, get frustrated because I can't do it, and finally am forced to admit that they are not analogous. It's always a great regret to have to put away good material. But who knows, my file of rejected ideas might come in useful... one day.

Good analogies are usually relevant to listeners. For example, for assembly talks they might draw on contemporary youth culture.

Beware 'borrowed interest' When I was developing TV commercials, I was taught to be very wary of what is called 'borrowed interest'. This is where something irrelevant to the main message is used to gain attention. You might think that anything that makes people sit up and take notice is a good thing, but the problem is that people remember the 'borrowed interest' item but forget the message. The ideal is for the 'interest' to be inseparable from the message, so that remembering one means remembering the other.

For example, a short time ago I saw an activity where volunteers had to unscramble anagrams to make people's names.

Activity: Unscrambling anagrams of names

For example...

Nidael	→	Daniel
Mesaj	→	James
Rolettach	→	Charlotte

This seemed a fun activity – and I thought 'this name game would make an ideal start to an assembly about Jesus' name and why its meaning of "God to the rescue" is appropriate.'

However, when I asked the local minister to look through the resulting outline, he pointed out that unscrambling anagrams has very little to do with explaining about Jesus. He suggested instead this alternative:

Activity: Meanings of names
For example...
Andrew → 'Manly' Matthew → 'Gift of God' Sarah → 'Princess'
Link with next step: The name 'Jesus' also has a meaning – 'God to the rescue'

If this illustration is used, a typical comment afterwards might be:

'We had a man to take assembly and he said my name meant "manly" and that Jesus' name also meant something.'

However, if I had used the activity of unscrambling anagrams of names, the comment might have been more like:

'We had a man to take assembly and we had to unscramble anagrams and it was fun and then we went on to something different but I've forgotten what it was.'

Keep the Bible Some pupils have told me that they would much prefer to hear about Jesus doing miracles and overturning tables in the Temple than about the religious conversion of a modern-day celebrity – even though the latter might be thought to be more 'relevant'. Many Christian visitors to schools regularly use Bible readings from one of the more user-friendly translations, like the Good News version. A version which seems to be increasingly popular is *The Message*, a modern translation by Eugene Peterson.[9] Some schools workers make a point of showing the Bible whenever they quote from it – it acts as a visual aid emphasising the fact that Christians read the Bible.

Comments from experienced assembly-takers Here are some

quotes from people who have been particularly involved in talking to young people in schools:

'When you go up there, you are in a sense performing and being larger than life, but you've got to be true to yourself. Don't try and be Billy Connolly or Ben Elton when you're not.'

'Try to learn stories rather than reading them. Then you can look round the audience and use eye contact to keep them with you.'

'Visual aids are for the speaker, just as much as for the people listening. If you use them, you don't need notes, and they help you relax. They can also help you keep to time, because you're less likely to start waffling.'

'Be careful about going overboard with different illustrations for the same point. Pupils have limited attention spans, and each time you start a new illustration, they'll think you're making yet another point and may switch off, even though as the speaker you know that you're continuing the same point. If you've got a good illustration – for example a parable – then run with it and make it work hard to illustrate the point effectively by itself.'

'Don't try to make fun of teachers, school meals or other faiths. If you do, offence might be given.'

'I never set off for the school without taking its telephone number with me in case of emergency.'

'Read prayers if you are using them – for some reason it is much easier for people to accept them that way.'

'I try not to use long quotations – there's something about them that turns people off. The only time I use quotes now is if they are short soundbites. If they're good soundbites, then it can be worthwhile repeating them.'

'I know that not everyone would agree with me, but I would be very careful about asking the children to do something like a Mexican wave as I will not do anything that teachers in the school would not do.'

'I never have any keys or money that could distract me if I were to put my hands in my trouser pockets.'

'Keep a resource file – and every time you read or hear anything that you think might be suitable for an assembly, put it in the file. Then when it comes to preparing an assembly in the future you won't be left thinking, "I read something that would fit really well – but which book was it in and which page...?"'

'One of the things God has really shown me over the last few years is the way Jesus talked to the Samaritan woman at the well. He didn't patronise her, he didn't talk down to her, yet he knew exactly what her life was like. That's how I try to be when I take an assembly.'

3

But I'm not confident at talking to young people

One of my nightmare situations goes something like this:

The man stands on the stage looking over five hundred faces, and he knows he hasn't done enough preparation. He doesn't really know what he's going to say; he wonders how long it will take before pupils see through him. He starts to read straight from some scrappy notes on A4 sheets. He's stumbling over words. He has to keep looking down to read, so there is no eye contact with pupils. But even though he's not looking at them, he can feel that they're getting restless, and are not held by his poorly thought-through prose. He loses his place and starts to repeat himself and waffle because he can't think of what he ought to say next. And now he can also feel teachers' eyes boring through him. His mind begins to dread their comments. There probably won't be open anger, just icy coldness, and a certain knowledge that they're thinking – 'we don't want this one again!..

The less confident a person is, the more likely he or she is to have imagined this type of situation. So how can one make sure that it doesn't happen in real life? One of the best ways is to get training and experience, and to get it in such a way that confidence is built up over time, rather than just going in at the deep end. This chapter suggests how that might be done.

How to be trained

One of the best ways is to shadow and learn from others who are experienced in taking Christian assemblies. For example, this might be a full-time schools worker, or a local minister.

Richard, full-time worker with Christian Options in Peterborough Schools (CROPS), says this about how he trains people to do assemblies:

'I'll always offer to go with people new to doing schools work. The first few times they sit at the back watching...

→ **demonstration**

...then I suggest they read a book on how to give a short talk and we talk about it...

→ **explanation**

...the first time they do an 'assembly', it should be to a harmless group. By harmless I mean their own kids, or a friend's kids...

→ **application**

...Someone needs to evaluate how they do. If I'm evaluating, I have to be honest, and sometimes I tell them to stick to prayer. People aren't always gifted in kids' work. They shouldn't feel obliged to do it – but if they don't do it, they should be encouraging someone else who can.'

→ **consolidation**

The key steps, then, are:
>   Demonstrate
>   Explain
>   Apply
>   Consolidate

I found the demonstration aspect to be very important – my confidence was greatly increased just by having more contact with the school environment. Low confidence can be due to fear of the unknown; when things become known and 'normal', then they become much easier to do. I increased my contact with schools by accompanying local full-time Christian schools workers. If there are some in your area, it should be possible to get their address via the Schools Ministry Network (see Part Three for contact details). An alternative is to ask a local minister or any other Christian who regularly goes into schools to take you with them. School chaplains – relatively common in independent schools – have huge experience in this area.

Another thing I found useful was to practise in front of a 'tame' audience. In order to get the most benefit out of the time that my 'volunteers' spent listening to me, I prepared a questionnaire for them to fill in – this is an easier way to receive feedback than just asking, 'So was it all right then?' Opposite is the questionnaire I used.

Principles underlying the questionnaire:

The first question asks for an overall rating of the assembly. A scale of 1-6 is used – this means that there is no mid-point, so the audience has to decide whether they think it's basically all right (by giving a rating of 4 or above) or whether it's not (by giving a rating of 3 or below).

Question 2 asks for ratings for the three areas looked at in the last chapter. This helps show where most work needs to be done to improve the assembly.

To what extent was it thought-provoking?   To what extent was it easy to follow?

To what extent was the way it was put over interesting?

Question 3 asks what the main point of the assembly is. This provides a useful check. It ought to be the same as the learning objective – if it's not, then clearly the structure needs further work.

In question 5, I would ask adults to give any comments on theology – for example, does the assembly actually reflect Biblical ideas?

WHAT DID YOU THINK OF THE ASSEMBLY?

Your initials: _____

Assembly name: _____

Please answer the first three questions by circling one number.

1. What did you think of the assembly overall?

    Very poor   Excellent

    1   2   3   4   5   6

2. To what extent do you agree with the following statements about the assembly?

    Disagree   Agree

    'It made me think'   1   2   3   4   5   6

    'It was easy to follow'   1   2   3   4   5   6

    'The way it was put over   1   2   3   4   5   6
    was interesting'

3. What do you think was the main point of the assembly? (please write this down)

4. What parts of the assembly do you think worked well?

5. What parts of the assembly do you think could be improved?

Thank you for your help!

Training Seminars

If there are a large number of people interested in being trained at one time, seminars can be a sensible option, perhaps in addition to the personal experience gained by going to schools with an experienced worker. The best seminars are those that compress the Demonstrate-Explain-Apply-Consolidate process into a few hours.

There are various organisations who might be able to run seminars in your area. These include, for example, Scripture Union, Youth for Christ, Association of Christian Teachers, and CARE for Education. Contact details of these and other local groups are listed in Part Three of this book.

Correspondence Course

Another option is to take a correspondence course. Janet King, formerly Religious Education and Worship Development officer at the Association of Christian Teachers, has written a course 'School Worship That Works'. This is administered by St John's Extension Studies in Nottingham. Contact details are again in Part Three.

On-going training: the benefit of going in twos

Even when people are trained and know what they are doing, it may still better to go in pairs to school assemblies. That's the advice of Cameron, a youth worker at Holy Trinity Brompton church in London.

'One reason for going in twos is for training and feedback,' says Cameron. 'But it's also better spiritually. One can pray for the other, and provide encouragement. The senior youth worker and myself take it in turns to do the talk if we're leading assemblies.'

My first assembly – a personal experience

I have never been a teacher, and could not claim to be particularly confident about speaking to young people. If you are in a similar position, I hope this 'countdown' to the first assembly that I took at a local secondary school might be of some encouragement. It's given as an example, not a model; being self-employed, I was able to be more flexible about time than others might be.

Thirty days to go

The date of my first assembly is confirmed and the school have given me the 'theme for the week'; all I need to do now is to work out my content, structure, and presentation method.... hard work!

Just as I'm about to start work on preparing the assembly, I start to think what a good idea it would be to put off doing anything, and instead have a cup of tea. But I know that this would be a recipe for doing nothing, and I pray: 'Heavenly Father, please guide my preparation for this assembly, so that the young people will learn something of you, even though I'm weak. Amen.' I start to look up Bible passages relevant to the school's theme, trying to understand the context so as not to misapply the key verses. Miscellaneous bits of advice float across my mind – 'get it right, get it across'; 'the essential for any Christian talk is prayer'; 'remember to "state, explain, illustrate, apply"' ...it's quite some time before I manage to come up with a first draft.

Twenty days to go

I'm always rather nervous about asking favours, but nevertheless I pluck up courage to call on my vicar. 'I haven't led an assembly before and I'd like to try out the idea that I've been working on. Is there are chance I could do this with you – and with your son too, as he's the right age for the assembly I'll be leading?'

Nineteen days to go

I perform my assembly to the vicar and his son, to whom I give lavish rewards of chocolate. They fill in my questionnaires – unfortunately the vicar's son thought the assembly had a different point to the one I was actually trying to get across. I need to do some serious rewriting...

Fourteen days to go

The local full-time Christian schools worker is leading an assembly at the school, and I go with her – it's the ninth or tenth assembly at which I've been an observer. Before the pupils arrive, she reminds me, 'Don't be intimidated by the size of the pupils.' I'm slightly surprised at this comment – I'm over six foot myself, and don't intend to be intimidated by teenagers ten years younger than me. However, when they come in, hundreds of them, looking as though they own the place, I know what she means. I find myself feeling quite glad to be able to stand inconspicuously along one side of the hall.

The simplicity and directness of her assembly makes me think the talk I'm planning could be too complicated. Looking round the school hall reminds me that there must be a real range of ability here, and I need to be speaking to everyone.

Thirteen days to go

I tell the 'Home Group' to which I belong about the assembly, and it's added to the list of prayer needs. As we break up, the Group's host says it would be no problem for me to practise my revised assembly with her children.

Twelve days to go

I visit the school again for a 'normal' assembly led by a teacher. I arrive early so that I have a chance to work out where I'm going to stand for my own assembly, and also to check out the acoustics. Like most schools, there are no microphones or PA system: I'll have to speak up.

This is all seems a lot of work – but I suppose I should expect it as it's the first assembly that I've led.

Seven days to go

After an early supper with the hosts of my Home Group, I ask the parents and three girls to sit at one end of the lounge, whilst I stand at the other.

Just after I have started my talk, a friend of one of the girls calls round to play. When she hears what's happening, she runs home to ask her mother for permission to join in – her family is Muslim – and then sits right at the front listening. The unexpected increase in audience is all good experience.

When I've finished, I hand out mounds of chocolate as a 'thank-you'. As soon as I'm back home, I look through the questionnaires that they all filled in for me – the scores are reasonable, but I note that one of the children has written 'Needs more confidence'.

Five days to go

I send the assembly co-ordinator an outline of what I'm intending to say (it's my sixth draft). It takes about an hour-and-a-half to write it down, type a covering letter, and post it off. I suppose that any sort of voluntary work should be expected to take up a fair amount of time.

Four days to go

It's a boiling hot Saturday, and I sit in some friends' garden and practise the assembly again. They advise me to cut down the length of time where I'm just talking, and make more of the illustrations. It's such an obvious comment – how come I didn't spot it myself, even though I know perfectly well what I'm aiming at?

My friends say they'll pray for the assembly too…

Two days to go

Still thinking about how to cut down my talk. When the other people working in the office have gone home, I lock myself in the toilet and practise in front of the mirror.

One day to go

As previously arranged, I call on the local full-time Christian schools worker and perform the assembly. She makes some very useful suggestions, and promises to come to the school and see how I do.

In the evening my girlfriend rides round to my house on her motorbike and patiently listens to me running through the assembly yet again. There's no doubt that it's greatly improved since my first drafts, and she tells me that I seem much more confident. I give a second rendition, this time taping it. We then replay the tape and comment on it, discussing small things that could be still be improved further. After a final run-through, I feel sure about what I'm going to say and exactly how I'm going to say it.

Two hours to go

Unbelievably, I forgot to switch on my alarm, and I wake up later than planned! Fortunately I still arrive at the school in plenty of time.

Half an hour to go

I report to the Head of Lower School whom I haven't previously met; I discover that she's seen me at meetings of the local Christian schools group (Christians and Tyneside Schools). I sit on the edge of a chair by her desk, feeling tense.

Six minutes to go

The hall is already filling up as I take my stand along the side wall. The local schools worker has come to support me as she promised; I feel more grateful to see a familiar face than I might have expected.

Four minutes to go

The Deputy Head of Year comes over to me. 'The pianist hasn't turned up. You don't play the piano, do you?' I look faintly aghast, and reply 'I'm afraid my talents don't stretch to that'.

'Oh well… ah, here he comes after all'.

Two minutes to go

Swing low, sweet chariot is belted out on the piano, with minimal singing accompaniment from the 300 twelve- and thirteen-year-olds.

Five seconds to go

The Deputy says, 'Thank you, that was very nice everybody. And now I'd like to introduce you to Richard. Those amongst you who are most observant might have spotted him the week before last when he visited an assembly, and today he's actually going to take one. So…'

One second to go

My heart is pounding and I feel keyed-up and ready. I know what I'm going to say. The Deputy finishes his sentence: 'So it's over to you, Richard,' and I walk onto centre-stage and start to speak…

* * *

If *you* are on stage

That was my experience. What about you?

If you take an assembly, this advice might be helpful for when you start to speak.

Coping with an elastic time constraint

Giving a short talk can be much more challenging than making a long speech, particularly when the time might be cut from ten to five minutes because some of the pupils arrive late.

One assembly I attended recently was going well when, in the middle of a solo song which was to finish off the assembly, the bell rang for the first lesson. As an observer, I could sense the shift in the teachers' attitudes. They began to look at their watches, and started to glance at each other rather than being fixed on the person taking the assembly. The pupils also began to get a little restless. The whole assembly had been carefully timed, but a delay in assembling the pupils had been enough to upset the balance. There is an opposite problem; at one assembly I led I unexpectedly found that there was to be no singing and there were no notices, leaving me an extra five minutes to fill. I started to pause dramatically between sentences and put my final comments into slow-motion, but even so I couldn't fill all the gap. The pupils were dismissed early – this wasn't a big problem, but nor was it ideal from the point of view of those responsible for ensuring pupils are supervised.

Some good advice given to me is to time individual sections of the assembly during preparation, and to have plans for shortening or lengthening sections. This helps flexibility.

Remembering what you've said to whom

'Can you remember if I've already told this group the story of Zaccheus?' This is not the sort of question to be asking teachers a minute before the start of assembly. A written record of what you've said, when, and to whom, is invaluable. It's all the more useful because year groups don't stay static – Year 7 this year will be Year 8 next year and so on. It can catch out the unwary!

One idea is to have an 'emergency' assembly prepared in case your records let you down and you suddenly find that you are confronted with pupils who have already heard what you were planning to say. The 'emergency' material should not have been used before, and should not require any special props or preparation.

Turning interest into over-excitement

A schools worker in London explained how he had regularly asked a local school if he could take Christian assemblies. At first the school was wary, but finally – after four years – he was invited in. A short time after he took his first assembly, another group of Christian visitors also came in. Their assembly was action-packed and wound up the children into a high state of excitement. They were very difficult for the teachers to manage afterwards. As a direct result, no more visitors were allowed in. John now faces another four years before the school is ready to risk inviting Christian visitors again.

Avoiding jargon

Another big issue is talks that become confusing, without the speaker ever realising it. Words like 'grace' can be meaningless to children who know nothing about Christianity.

Dealing with volunteers

It can often be a good idea to involve pupils in an assembly – it creates interest as well as helping to break down the barrier between speaker and audience. This is particularly the case if the speaker learns and uses the volunteers' names.

In primary schools, one point to watch is that smaller children may find some instructions hard to handle – it might be sensible to ask for volunteers from an older year group, depending on what you would like them to do.

In secondary schools it is generally harder to get volunteers. I have had the experience of nobody coming forward when I asked; there was an awkward fifteen seconds (it seemed longer!) before two people did eventually 'volunteer'. This was partly because of the age-group (Year 9), partly because it was the first assembly I'd led with the group, so I had yet to develop the trust and credibility which make it easier to get a response, and partly because of mistakes in the way I'd gone about it. Here are some ideas I was given to help avoid similar problems:

- With older age-groups, it can be better to ask for people to help with an activity (perhaps giving some details of what they'll do) than to ask generally for 'volunteers'.
- Ask the first pupils who arrive for assembly to help, so that you know you've covered your needs for volunteers before the assembly starts.
- If you're having to 'volunteer' people from the front during assembly, the way you ask is important. Rather than giving an option 'would you mind standing at the front being a volunteer?', try the more assertive, 'I need two people to help – you and you.'
- Another idea is to ask a teacher before assembly for names of pupils who could help. At the appropriate moment, pretend you have everyone's names in a hat, and then apparently 'pull out' the names you've been given.
- If other people are with you, you can use them as helpers

instead of reluctant pupils.

- If there is no stage, you could stand in a centre aisle amongst pupils; if this is the case, you might not need specific volunteers, but could just use the people sitting close to you.
- Some schools workers to whom I've talked give a prize to every volunteer (for example a large Mars bar). They claim this has good results in encouraging volunteers on their subsequent visits!

4

...But how do I approach schools?

Make it easy for the head teacher to say 'yes'...

There would have been no point in writing this book if schools were generally closed to Christian visitors. Recently, I was very interested in the results of a small survey carried out by the Principal of a local college,[1] to which 121 of his colleagues responded. Not one of them ruled out the possibility of Christian visitors leading assemblies. At the same time, many were wary; it was quite common for the head teachers to expect to be informed about the content of assemblies to be taken by first-time visitors. A smaller number also expected visitors to have references from other head teachers, or to have references from churches they knew.

Christian visitors need to reassure this wariness on the part of head teachers if they are really to play a part in providing 'broadly Christian' assemblies. This chapter tries to give a step-by-step guide to how to make it easy for schools to say 'yes' to an offer of assistance.

Flowchart

This flowchart draws on interviews with full-time schools workers and teachers, and gives a suggested process for contacting schools.

You're a Christian wanting to offer support to a local school for 'broadly Christian' assemblies. It is something that you've been praying about.

YES

Do you have relevant experience?

NO

Consider getting some training

Decide with which age groups you feel more comfortable (primary? secondary?)

Is there someone else who would go to schools with you and support you in leading assemblies?

● Establish what the needs are in local schools by talking to teachers, governors, etc that you know.
● Look to complement existing work.
● Are there schools attended by young people with whom you already have links and whom you would like to support?

Select school(s) to contact.

Ask any existing contacts in the selected schools for advice and to have an informal word with the head teacher.

Ring the school secretary to (a) find out who to speak to about assemblies – usually the head teacher, and (b) to obtain a copy of the school's 'collective worship' policy, if there is one.

Write to the head teacher, introducing yourself and respectfully offering your support.

Follow up with a phone call to determine interest and, if appropriate, to arrange a meeting.

Meet for around fifteen minutes with the head teacher or assembly co-ordinator:
● Dress formally, as you would for an assembly.
● Aim to understand fully the school's approach to 'collective worship'.
● Discuss the content of your proposed first assembly.
● Discuss frequency of visits (the ideal is sustained involvement, if mutually acceptable).
● Leave references that could be followed up if desired by the assembly co-ordinator.
● Discuss possible dates.
● Confirm any agreements in writing.

Visit ordinary assemblies to see what happens and perhaps to be introduced to pupils and staff.

Take assembly.

Ask for feedback – probably from the teacher who invited you – and use this to improve the assembly.
Arrange time for next assembly, if convenient.

Record what you said, when, and to which year group.

Look for further ways to become involved.

In more detail...

Let's look more closely at some of the boxes:

1. Are you offering long-term support to schools?

> You're a Christian wanting to offer support to a local school for 'broadly Christian' assemblies. It is something that you've been praying about.

A crucial question to consider is: are you just offering 'one-off' support, or is it going to be something that you keep up for a long period?

Richard, the schools worker at Christian Options for Peterborough Schools, says, 'I would refuse to do assemblies on a "hit-and-run basis". It must keep raining to get the ground moist – water runs off a dry surface! I'll ask to do a minimum of one or two assemblies a term at any school I go to.'

This view is one that I have heard again and again – sustained contact with schools is the ideal. Another schools worker says, 'It would be very easy for my diary to be completely full of different assembly visits – but these only have value if they are part of some ongoing programme... I aim to visit primary and first schools every half-term; middle schools about the same.'

2. Primary or secondary schools?

> Decide with which age groups you feel more comfortable (primary? secondary?)

Primary schools...? One Baptist minister told me: 'I do find the primary school context easier – you can go in and be flexible. It's more difficult in secondary schools – it's more formal.' I know what he means. Compared to being on a stage addressing hundreds of secondary pupils, it is less intimidating to talk in a much smaller room filled with much smaller people. Moreover, as another minister put it: 'Kids get to be much more "cool" by the age of fifteen' – and I think that by 'cool', he means that they do not seem to be that responsive.

...or secondary schools? Secondary schools may be more demanding – but are the needs greater? It's more likely that they will be short of staff willing to lead broadly Christian 'collective worship'; shortage of space can force secondary schools into having numerous assemblies led by different people, rather than having the whole school together and only needing one person to lead. It may also be true that, since Christian assemblies are less common in many secondary schools than in primary schools, there is more impact when they do happen.

So is it better to concentrate support on secondary schools, or primary schools? The answer to that question will depend upon the individual situation.

3. Utilise existing contacts

> Ask any existing contacts in the selected schools for advice and to have an informal word with the head teacher.

Contacts are key! The children's worker at a Pentecostal church wrote to me to say: 'One of our members is a school governor, and was the means of getting me into the Junior and Infants Schools to take assemblies...'

Chance contacts can be just as useful as people well known to the church. A pastor in London says, 'A teacher visited our church on the occasion of the baptism of one of her pupils. As a result of her visit, I have recently been invited to do assemblies in a local senior school. Up until this, we had done very little really.'

4. Make it easy for the headteacher to say 'yes'

> Write to the head teacher, introducing yourself and respectfully offering your support.

Opposite is a sample letter, based on ones that have been written in the past. You may find it helpful to draw on it if you are going to contact schools yourself:

Principles underlying the sample letter:

Make it clear that you are a Christian Head teachers, like many people in responsible positions, want to avoid surprises. The sample letter makes it very clear where the writer is coming from – she's a Christian who, if invited, would talk about what Christians believe.

Make it clear what you are offering There is a range of support that Christians can offer to schools, and head teachers should not be left to guess about what 'support' is being offered. Greg, a pastor, told me: 'When I offered "support", I made it clear that I would initially limit this to being regularly involved in classroom activities. I did this so that I felt more comfortable and at ease with all those involved, before I came to take assemblies. I would want to recommend this approach.' In the sample letter, on the other hand, the writer obviously feels able to offer assistance in leading assemblies straight up.

Another minister explained to me that he had offered to assist in whatever way the school would like. This might be a rather open-ended commitment for individual Christians! He said: 'We wrote as a fellowship to all our local schools. We expressed to the heads that we appreciated the task they had, and were praying for them. If we could help them in any way to please contact us. The result of those letters is regular assemblies at three primary schools and involvement with the Christian Union at one school'.

Make use of your previous experience 'Have done, can do' is the attitude some headteachers will have about visitors. In other words, if you can show that you have been welcomed time after time by other schools, it's more likely that you will be considered a reliable person to take assemblies.

Dear Mr Bloggs,

Support for assemblies

Many schools find that Christian visitors can play a useful part in their assembly programme, and I was wondering if Sometown School was looking for further involvement from local Christian churches. Mrs Jones, a governor, gave me your name as head teacher.

I am a member of St Paul's church (Church of England) which is about half a mile from Sometown School. Our former vicar occasionally took an assembly at your school; however, as you may be aware, our parish has now been joined with a number of others, and time has not allowed the new vicar to maintain the link.

I would be very happy to offer my support for assemblies. My experience of leading 'collective worship' comes mainly from attending and learning from assemblies taken by John Smith, a local full-time Christian schools worker. I have also led four assemblies myself in Othertown Primary school; topics included 'faith' and 'Easter'. The head teacher has kindly agreed to act as a referee for me.

In any assembly, I would aim at an engaging and sensitive presentation of a Christian message. I would be very happy to fit in with a theme for the week, if appropriate. I would also intend to check my proposed material in advance with you.

If I may, I will telephone you over the next few days about this, and perhaps arrange a short meeting with you. In the meantime, please don't hesitate to contact me at any time on 0181 000 000.

I look forward to speaking with you.

Yours sincerely,

Jane Smith (Mrs)

Consistent with this principle, Christian groups that contact a number of schools sometimes produce leaflets that give an indication of their 'fruit', so that new schools can find out what type of 'tree' they are.

A Youth for Christ leaflet, which lists the seven schools in which the local worker is involved, uses quotes from teachers along the lines of...

> 'I have been very impressed...He has brought interest and enthusiasm while making them think'
>
> John Smith, Head of Humanities, Arden High School

A leaflet for another Christian 'Schools Support group' has the following quotes:

> 'The assemblies and lessons were thought provoking and challenging. Staff and pupils were impressed. I believe you are a valuable support to schools.'
>
> Fred Brown, Head of Year, Moor School
> (following a series of Year 10 lessons and various assemblies)

> 'You were very well received by the boys and girls, your thought-provoking approach and quiet authority has been deeply appreciated by a number of pupils.'
>
> Mr J Bloggs, Headteacher, Valley School
> (following a number of class discussions on Hallowe'en)

In the sample letter, direct quotes like the ones above were not used since they may seem too self-satisfied (but they do work well in a separate leaflet!). Instead, the letter mentioned a school previously visited – and the willingness of that school to renew its invitation more than once will convey a positive message to the recipient. Moreover, the head teacher of that school is given as a possible reference.

References can be particularly useful for visitors without an established reputation. An elder of a city church, related to New Frontiers International, says, 'Because we're a new church, schools are wary. We are helped by being able to give a well-known local Christian schools worker as a reference.'

When it comes to following up the letter, the best time to telephone teaching staff is half-an-hour before school starts, during lunch, or just after school. Head teachers tend to be easier to contact of at other times of the day – although they often have full diaries.

5. Meet the key contacts at the school

> Meet with the head teacher or assembly co-ordinator

An Anglican priest-in-charge wrote to me that: 'Clergy are welcome when good relationships are established with the teaching staff.' An important way of forming such relationships can be an introductory meeting. The meeting might be with the head teacher, assembly co-ordinator, or another member of the school's Senior Management Team (SMT).

A college Principal points out that when he first meets potential visitors, they need to bridge a 'credibility gap'. As far as he is concerned, the dress of a visitor increases or decreases that gap. Someone who comes in wearing jeans or shorts would have a hard job to prove that they are 'reliable'. The Principal's suggestion, therefore, is that dress should be appropriate to the school – and if pupils wear a uniform then that will usually mean a tie for men and an equivalent standard of dress for women. This would be the case both for a meeting with staff, and for an assembly.

6. Understand what normally happens in assemblies

> Visit ordinary assemblies to see what happens, and perhaps to be introduced to pupils and staff.

The old-style school assembly was 'hymn-reading-prayer'. But what goes on today in schools that you might visit?

There will often be a talk; in secondary schools this will probably last less than ten minutes, but might be longer in primary schools. Singing hymns and listening to music seem to take place in a fairly small minority of secondary schools, although singing is common in primary. Church schools are fairly likely to have prayers and Bible readings; non-church schools (particularly secondary) are less likely to have them.

If you visit a school before taking an assembly, it can be a chance to make contact with Christian members of staff. One former teacher that I met said that he used to feel rather aggrieved when visitors came in, assumed they were the only Christian influence on the school, took an assembly, and then left again without ever seeking to meet him, co-ordinate with him, or support him in his daily witness. He would encourage visitors to identify and make contact with Christians already working in a school before beginning something new.

It's useful to be introduced to any teachers who will be leading assemblies around the time that you will be taking yours, as this can avoid unfortunate repetition of material. You may have found the best ever idea for an assembly in a book, but it will be not be as wonderful to the pupils if they heard exactly the same thing from exactly the same book the day before.

7. Talk to teachers about assemblies

> Ask for feedback – probably from the teacher who invited you.

One way that a school gives 'feedback' on a visitor's assembly is the blunderbuss method of either continuing or cancelling their invitation to the visitor. More detailed feedback can be gained through questionnaires filled in by teachers (or even pupils selected by a teacher). This not only gets you feedback, but it also shows that you are concerned about what the school thinks. A questionnaire for teachers that I have used is shown opposite.

A good time to talk with teachers about how the assembly went can be over coffee in the staff room before or after assembly;

WHAT DID YOU THINK OF THE ASSEMBLY?

Your initials: _____

Assembly name:_____

Please answer the first three questions by circling one number.

1. What did you think of the assembly overall?

	Very poor				Excellent	
	1	2	3	4	5	6

2. To what extent do you agree with the following statements about the assembly?

	Disagree				Agree	
'It made the pupils think'	1	2	3	4	5	6
'It was easy for the pupils to follow'	1	2	3	4	5	6
'The way it was put over was interesting'	1	2	3	4	5	6

3. What do you think was the main point of the assembly? (please write this down).

4. What parts of the assembly do you think worked well?

5. What parts of the assembly do you think could be improved?

Thank you for your help!

whether you are invited or not depends on the nature of the school and of the people.

7. Further ways to serve schools and young people

> Look for further ways to become involved.

There are many ways that 'support for schools' can be expressed. John, a schools worker in the North-East, believes that over time visiting Christians will want to do more than the 'God-slot'; they will want to build relationships with the pupils they speak to, and further the Christian witness within the school. In what ways can this be done?

Some Christians offer to act as a resource when it comes to planning assembly themes. For example, they can suggest suitable Biblical passages to illustrate topics that the school intends to cover, or recommend relevant Christian resource books. The Association of Christian Teachers (ACT) is keen to promote the idea that a church or group of churches 'sponsor' Christian resource books for schools.

One minister says: 'I have given an after-school talk to all the teachers at one school on how to tell Bible stories.'

Another idea comes from an Anglican minister: 'I attend one school on a Wednesday morning for half-an-hour (modern) hymn singing with about seventy children and this provides a good opportunity to become known by the children. The headmaster is welcoming and gives the opportunity to talk or pray with the children. They also come to the church for Christmas Festival.'

* * *

In the last section of this chapter, let's look at ways of dealing with some of the reservations that schools may feel about Christian visitors. First, a real life experience...

A schools worker tells the story of a school that refused to accept his offer of assisting with Christian assemblies because 'if we let you take an assembly, then we'll have to let others in too. You may be all right, but others might not be; so the fairest thing is not to invite anyone.'

The schools worker recognised that the core of this objection was their fear that no visitor could really be trusted – including him.

The school does now let him take assemblies. How did this reversal happen?

He puts it down to the fact that he was able to prove that he *could* be trusted. He did this by demonstrating the substantial links that he already had with pupils at the school, through after-school events and Christian holidays. These links were evidence that he was fully reliable. As a result, the school now feel comfortable about inviting him – and their earlier argument based on 'fairness' has been quietly forgotten.

Dealing with objections

Imagine that you're now sitting in the waiting room of a head teacher's office, clasping your hands and suddenly feeling nervous as you contemplate the meeting ahead of you. You're about to discuss how you could contribute in the area of 'collective worship'. Supposing the Head has all sorts of objections that weren't mentioned on the telephone? What are you going to say?

It's easier to deal with such things if you've considered them in advance. Here are suggested ways of meeting concerns that head teachers may have.

Objection: 'I'm not sure I want any Christian visitors at all – the last lot that visited the school, despite being briefed about what was permissible, used the opportunity to evangelise in a way that was insensitive to students of other faiths.'

Answer: To ensure an approach in line with your policy on collective worship, I would check the content with you in advance were I to be invited to take an assembly.

*

Objection: 'A few years ago we had a bad experience with a visitor who over-ran his time and who bored the children. I don't want a repeat of that.'

Answer: *I appreciate the need for visitors to do a very good job. I would be very happy for you to follow up a reference from a respected schools worker, who has seen the type of assembly that I take.*

*

Objection: 'I hear on the grapevine that there were complaints from parents after a Christian group got the children in a nearby school really wound up during an assembly. I don't want to risk something like that.'

Answer: *You are right to want reassurance. Let me say firstly that any assembly that I take is always educational, not playing on emotions. Secondly, may I encourage you to check with some of the teachers at other schools where I've led assemblies in the past, and then been invited back?*

*

Objection: 'I just don't know much about your type of churches – how do I know that you're not from one of those cults?'

Answer: *I have references here from... (someone who would have standing in the school – for example another head teacher, a known schools worker, and so on).*

*

Objection: 'I'm not sure we need your input – a local vicar already comes in once a year.'

Answer: *I have already spoken with the vicar in question, and we have agreed that we would co-ordinate what we would do in assemblies. By both being involved, we will be able to increase the amount of support that visiting Christians are able to offer you.*

5

...But I don't have enough time or support

Some of you reading this book are likely to be paid Christian workers, whether as ministers, members of church staff, youth workers, or in another capacity. If you are, then you are part of the group that most frequently visits schools to lead Christian assemblies. Because this group is so crucial, this chapter suggests ways to help you do more.

If you are not a paid Christian worker – perhaps you are someone whose job allows them the flexibility to take assemblies, or maybe you are retired – then please do read on, even if you find some parts are less immediately relevant to you.

One of the questions that I asked when I first started looking into assemblies was: why are some churches heavily involved with assisting schools, whilst others aren't? (By 'church' I mean ministers, any other church staff, and congregation) Is there perhaps some secret here? I decided to ask church leaders for their views.

I didn't just ask a few church leaders, but hundreds. I wrote to 500 church leaders[1] enclosing a questionnaire, and just over 300 sent it back completed – a response rate of over 60% (this is relatively high).

I spent hours sifting through the mounds of completed questionnaires, searching for the secret of being able to do more assemblies. If only I could look hard enough and long enough, surely I would find it. At last I did. Churches assist with more assemblies if... if they put a higher priority on it. It's very straightforward – 'where there's a will, there's a way.'

This obvious but crucial fact was not the only thing revealed by my hours of going through questionnaires. It also showed, somewhat to my surprise, that ministers see themselves as doing the brunt of the work of visiting schools as representatives of the Christian faith. Of the 196 respondents to my survey who said that someone from their church was involved in visiting schools to lead assemblies (apart from teachers[2]), the 'someone' was usually a minister.

Type of people who visit schools to lead assemblies

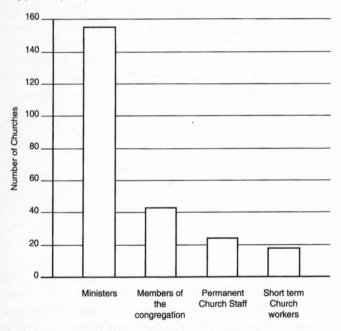

Sample: 196 Churches (mainly evangelical) that assist with assemblies.
Note: 'Permanent church staff' excludes ministers.

The following story incorporates a number of the comments and ideas generated by my survey, and I hope it may give you some practical ideas on how to make effective use of your own time, as well as how to help others become involved.

'I'll get round to it next month'

This is the Journal of Reverend A N Other, who is facing the common problems of not enough time and not enough resources...

January

We talked about schools at the church council today, and we agreed that they are high on our agenda – but there are other things that are even higher. We just don't seem to have enough time for all the important things. It'd be great if lots of people from the congregation were taking the initiative and I just had to equip them, but... amongst our fellowship there doesn't seem to be anyone with the time, ability or willingness to help schools. I'll try and do something myself – I'll get round to it next month.

February

I really will get round to it next month.

March

Nothing's happened so far, but I really really will get round to it next month. Must remember to pray.

April 3rd

Just had a surprise call from Jane, who moved away from the church a few years ago. Believe it or not, she's now a co-leader of a team from Youth With A Mission (YWAM), and she wants to bring her team of young people here for a week. I told her it'd be great to have them, and that of course we could accommodate them in our homes during the visit. Yes, there's several things we could use her team for: Sunday school work, and maybe an event at the old people's home ...

April 5th

After the mid-week prayer meeting, we thought that the visit of the team would actually be a good opportunity to push on a few doors in schools. I must admit this wasn't something I'd thought about in advance – but why not?

Everyone else on the church council agreed that I should be the one to approach the school – 'you'll have that bit more credibility,' they said, 'as the person with a recognised position in the church.' We prayed about this new step...

April 15th

The first thing I did was to find out what other churches are already doing – there's no point in treading on each other's toes. The Anglican minister occasionally takes an assembly at the school, so we agreed to synchronise our teaching plan in an attempt to maximise the effect we can have.

The second thing was to think about follow-up. On-going is better than one-off; what can be done long term?

I talked to my friend Mike – we've worked on joint events before, and I've heard that he's very good with children during the services at his Baptist church. We've agreed to work together on taking regular assemblies after the main YWAM event. I'm not a Baptist myself, but in schools everything has to 'broadly Christian', so I think it'll work out well.

Now at last I can write that introductory letter to the headteacher...

April 18th

I wasn't entirely sure of what response I'd get when I telephoned the headteacher today: as it turns out, she is very enthusiastic about the prospect of the team visiting. It's a big advantage that Jane is a former pupil of the school. Contacts, contacts...

I also asked if the team could do something in lunchtimes too. No problem. The team are booked for three lunch time events as well as four assemblies.

May

Getting ready for the team's visit...

June 14th

This week has been brilliant! I went with the team into the school on Tuesday. You could have heard a pin drop during the assembly – teachers told me they had never seen assemblies so quiet and attentive. The team gave a mime presentation of the gospel from Creation to the Cross in just over ten minutes. They had been rehearsing it for a long time – and the preparation showed. There were no requests to come forward or anything like that – it was purely a presentation. The lunchtime events also went very well – about a hundred pupils attended.

June 18th

We had a review of the team's visit, and everyone felt very positive about the school part of it. The team probably helped the Christian Union at the school. At that age, young Christians can feel vulnerable, and the team gave a little bit of support and 'street cred'. And if nothing else, all the pupils saw that there is another side to the church, that it can be exciting, that it's not just old ladies in funny hats.

We feel we've also built our relationship with the school. I'm now going to lead an assembly every fortnight, along with Mike – they were very happy for two ministers to work together like this.

July

Mike and I took our first assembly this morning. We managed to hold the pupils' attention, and the Head said she was very happy with what we'd done.

August

Holiday!

September 29th

The autumn term assemblies are going well – but I can't deny that the preparation is hard work. It would be great if we could employ a part-time worker – he or she could also help with our church youth work...

October 25th

Still thinking and praying about getting a worker. I quite like the idea of a young person coming in for a short period – say a year. The cost would be quite reasonable, it could bring in fresh ideas, and should be good experience for whoever is appointed.

October 28th

I talked about a worker with Mike. He suggested that it would be even better if there was a long-term worker who would really be able to build up relationships with young people over a number of years. He's right, of course – but could we afford the higher pay that a long-term worker would need?

Mike also pointed out the amount of time it will take to get things up and running – it takes time and effort to recruit somebody, and then train them up. Perhaps it's too much for me to take on at this stage.

November 1st

Praise God! A real answer to prayer... We're going to work in partnership with a local group concerned with schools – Christians in Sometown Schools. They are going to find a worker, train him or her up, and handle all the administration. Our part of the arrangement is that Mike's Baptist church and my church together are going to pay the person for two mornings a week to work in local schools.

December

The Christmas assembly that Mike and I prepared was well received – at least young people are already familiar with some of the imagery of Christmas, even if they're not clear about the underlying message. It would have been great to have had a team with us to do a drama or something, but still, it went well...

January

A good start to the year – the new part-time worker has been appointed. Christians in Sometown Schools had thought about placing adverts in *Christianity* magazine and *Youthwork*, but in the end we felt that the right person was on the doorstep – Helen, who has been attending the Baptist church for years. The reason she became interested in schools was because of Mike and me starting to lead assemblies – it's funny how once something starts, the momentum builds up. The way she's financed is fairly creative – as well as being paid by the two churches to work two mornings in schools, she's also got a part-time job with someone from Mike's congregation for a couple of days a week which pays her enough to live on.

Helen's brimming with enthusiasm, but she is a bit short of experience. The last thing I would want would be for her to not live up to teachers' expectations, and close schools to other Christian visitors...

February

Christians in Sometown Schools have given good reports of Helen's progress through the training period. I always knew she'd be fine!

We went to the Prince's Trust with a specific project for a video projector. Representatives of the Trust came to look around and meet us, and then contributed £400 towards the cost. Helen is delighted at the extra equipment.

March

It's all going well...

April

It's all going very well...

May

It's definitely all going very well...

June 3rd

Ah, rather a bombshell this morning. Helen has decided to go to

Bible College. Her imminent departure has suddenly made me aware of the gap that exists between Helen's work and the rest of the church. Frankly, it's been easiest for her to just go and do the work rather than try to galvanise other volunteers from the church to get involved. Now that Helen is no longer going to be here, however, we have a problem. I see now that perhaps it hasn't been going that well after all.

July

Helen has had a change of heart (thank goodness) and will be going next year rather than this year. Still, it's clear that we must work on getting more support from the congregation, so that contact with schools can continue even without Helen. How can we do this? Most people seem so busy – I don't know of anyone who would be even remotely interested ....

September

Two people from my congregation have agreed to help Helen on a regular basis. One is a housewife called Barbara, the other works flexi-time at the Sun Alliance, and fits in an assembly before starting work. To begin with, they're just going to pray for the work and help in small ways, like saying the prayer at the end of assembly, moving puppets and so on. But they've both got a real heart for the work, and I'm sure they'll soon feel more confident and start to take leading roles in assemblies themselves over the next term or so.

We're now praying for the schools work in our fortnightly church prayer meetings, as well as having a 'care group' regularly praying for Helen and the people who help her.

November

A retired couple have now volunteered to help in the schools work as well! Their grandchildren have started going to the primary school, and they came to me asking how they could support the school – they knew through our prayers at the church meetings that we had contacts with it. The husband was a teacher for thirty years, and with so much experience of dealing with children I think the school will be very pleased to have his help.

December

Helen and her 'team' have prepared a brilliant Christmas assembly complete with a drama acted by her team of four volunteers. This has led to invitations to more schools...

*

I hope that some of the ideas in this 'Journal' might be useful to you. Early on it talked of the visit of a team from a Christian organisation. This type of visit can be a useful support to schools – as well as to churches struggling with a lack of available people. Overleaf is a sample letter which could be used to introduce a similar idea.

This letter – like the incidents in the story – is based on the experience and advice of the hundreds of people who took part in my survey. My thanks go to them for the time they put into filling them in the complicated questionnaire I sent them!

15th April

Dear Mr Bloggs,

Support for assemblies: visit of the Christian Theatre Company.

May we introduce an initiative that we hope will support your school in the area of assemblies?

As a group of local churches, our aim is to assist the provision of 'collective worship' of a broadly Christian character in schools. One of our initiatives is to organise a visit by the Christian Theatre Company in the last two weeks of January of next year.

The Christian Theatre Company is a top-flight professional group who communicate their Christian belief through drama. They have performed in over a hundred schools up and down the country, and we have had extremely positive feedback from those who have seen them, both from staff and especially young people. A list of headteachers willing to act as referees for the Christian Theatre Company is attached.

During their visit, the Company will be available to take part in and lead not only assemblies, but also RE classes, discussions, Christian Unions and drama workshops. There will be no charge for their time.

We would very much like to receive your reactions to the idea of using this group in your school. We will telephone you over the next few days; alternatively, please feel free to telephone either of us, or write to us at one of the addresses below.

We look forward to speaking to you.

Yours sincerely,

Revd A N Other   Revd S M Else

On behalf of:
<list of ministers who are co-ordinating their efforts towards schools, with addresses and phone numbers>

Attachment:
List of headteachers willing to act as referees for the Christian Theatre Company.

6

Developing a local Christian group concerned with assemblies and schools

The scene is the community room attached to a large church in the north of England. A group of casually dressed people is attending a regional seminar organised by Schools Ministry Network. In front of them stands a speaker who says, 'Many of you here are unpaid volunteers going into schools. What I'd like is for you to turn to the people around you and ask them how they got involved in schools work, and who's supporting them. Go!'

There is a silver-haired couple whose name badges distinguish them as Ken and Jennifer. Ken leans forward and says, 'We retired from teaching three years ago – thankfully – and this has been the means of releasing us into Christian work in schools. One does have some experience and feel for schools, and this has been used.

'We lead assemblies and also run Christian groups. Part of it stemmed from some young people who attended our church – they asked if we could help with a Christian group in their school, and things went from there. We also had an invitation from another teacher to support her.

'There are three of us at the moment – me, my wife Jennifer, and an unemployed lad. We make up Othertown Schools Support Team. We just make our own provision for an income, so to that extent there is no financial burden on anyone else. Our church though does have a real heart for young people, and gets behind us in all kinds of encouraging ways.'

Sitting nearby is a middle-aged lady with thick glasses. She says, 'I'm not the one going into schools actually – it's my husband. He used to work at a shop and had Wednesdays off, so he came along to the school where I worked – I'm a primary school teacher. Then he started to say he could do a good job of assemblies. He helped out, and eventually he was leading them. About a year ago he felt called to do this full-time. At first he went about with a schools worker, a very experienced one, but now he has his own patch and goes on his own. I've been supporting both of us through supply teaching, and the Lord has provided us with enough to live on'.

*

These personal histories illustrate how schools work can be supported 'informally'. It is also possible for more formal groups to support input into schools.

Some time ago I attended the Annual General Meeting of Christian Youth Ministries (CYM), a Christian group concerned with schools in the Ipswich area. I was struck by the range of their activity – assemblies, lessons, residential weekends, youth celebrations, road shows, running a drop-in centre, and more. The whole operation was on a much larger scale than the work of the individuals described above. One of the things making this possible is the greater fundraising impact of a 'formal' group. This Annual General Meeting was attended by well over a hundred supporters from different denominations, all channeling their concern for schools through CYM.

In the early 1980s I was at school at Ipswich and I remember a talk given by Nigel, CYM's first full-time worker. Since those days the ministry has grown considerably, with four workers now employed. Some of the lessons from their growth, and from other Christian groups I've interviewed, are :

1. Stay close to your supporters
2. Know where you are going
3. Ensure God is at the centre of what you do

As we look at these lessons in more detail, I hope that they might be useful for anyone concerned to develop an effective local Christian group concerned with assemblies and with schools generally.

1. Stay close to your supporters

In pursuit of developing their relationships with local churches, CYM has not been afraid of asking church leaders to join their advisory group and committee. This helps integrate them, and ensures they know the needs and opportunities being faced. The full-time worker at another group, Christian Options in Peterborough Schools (CROPS), says, 'We want local churches to "own" CROPS because then they finance it and pray for it; it's theirs.'

Nigel from CYM explains another idea: 'We have a monthly prayer meeting for the work of CYM, and we hold it in different churches each time. The minister publicises the prayer meeting to his congregation, but doesn't have to do anything else. We run the evening. We use our CYM video, we do the complete evening's programme. Then we all pray together for the work.' If two birds can be killed with one stone – prayer and communication – so much the better!

CYM has also developed a network of 'co-ordinators', one for each of the local churches in the area. This could be thought of as a biblical model – Exodus 18 provides an example of using networks rather than a few people trying to do everything themselves; Jethro advised Moses that dividing up the work amongst many means 'you will be able to endure' (18:23). In practice, local contacts can do the job of putting up publicity notices in the church (assuming agreement from the minister). They can act as immediate contacts for new people interested in the work, instead of the central co-ordinator having to do it all. They can also distribute letters to others in the congregation, cutting postage costs.

Other ideas include:
- Ask church leaders to interview a representative of the group for a few minutes during a service.
- Encourage 'Education Sundays' at local churches if they do

not already have one. These are ordinary Sunday services with special prayers for schools. There may also be an interview with or sermon from someone involved in schools work. Some churches in Ipswich give the collections on their 'Education Sunday' to CYM, as part of their practical response.

● Ask for a notice board giving information on the group to be put up in each local church.

● Always have available a high quality presentation about the work of the group. CYM has invested considerable time in presentations about its work. At first they used slides; more recently they have been videos.

● Keep supporters up-to-date with termly mailings. The mailings should be full of news and items for which prayer is requested.

2: Know where you are going

Several of the groups to which I have spoken have adopted a 'statement of belief' to show potential supporters the basic Christian position they stand for. They have also developed more specific objectives, such as:

Present the gospel to young people
Encourage Christian teachers
Exert a Christian influence on schools.

Opposite are some detailed ideas from existing groups about how those objectives could be met.

People are interested in an organisation that seems to be going somewhere, and lose interest when the organisation stagnates. If a Christian group concerned with schools seems to be making progress towards clear objectives, it's more likely to gain support. If, on the other hand, there's nothing to be excited about and no challenge to meet, the group will descend a downward spiral.

3: Ensure God is at the centre of what you do

Graham Hunt, administrator of Christians in Derbyshire Schools, believes that his organisation is 'all done on relationships'.

Objective 1. Present the gospel to young people
How can the objective be met?
- Train volunteers to lead assemblies and Christian Unions
- Finance schools workers
- Set-up a 'clearing house' system to administer and co-ordinate visits of Christians to schools
- Organise a Schools Conference on a topic of Religious Education for local 6th formers
- Encourage Christian Union members to go on residential weekends run by Christian organisations by offering vouchers towards the cost
- Organise inter-school Christian evangelism meetings and celebrations
- Establish a Christian drop-in centre for pupils to use after school hours
- Organise a road-show that pupils can go to after school hours, publicised via assemblies and Christian Unions
- Provide external pastoral support (for example, offer to be an 'independent listener') at a local private school

Objective 2: Encourage Christian Teachers
How can the objective be met?
- Regular prayer for and with teachers
- Hold annual worship events specifically for teachers
- Establish a resources centre for Religious Education teachers and people who take assemblies
- Produce a newsletter for local Christian teachers
- Hold regular meetings for teachers with a speaker to examine issues related to education

Objective 3: Exert a Christian influence on schools
How can the objective be met?
- Set up prayer groups for local schools
- Publicly speak out on Christian issues on education, and campaign locally
- Give each local school a £50 book voucher for Christian books
- Train school governors to be more effective as Christian governors

The most important relationship is with God.

'We're constantly seeking the Lord's guidance', says Graham. 'Our meetings are run as prayer meetings, not as business meetings.'

The executive committee holds early morning prayer meetings (7am) every half term. It's a time when they come together before God, and remind themselves of the need for a 'servant heart', as well as dealing with management issues.

* * *

Let's finish this chapter with some general thoughts on managing largely voluntary organisations.

Managing a voluntary group

1. 20% of people do 80% of the work. Therefore find the active 20% and get them involved.
2. If you ask people to do things and involve them, they will do more and more. If you ask them to do very little, they will do even less.

   One of the key reasons why people leave voluntary groups is because too little is done, not too much.
3. People who retire early are a good resource for voluntary groups.

   Compared to a few years ago, many people are now retiring early. Often they are able to take on new roles. Although in age terms they are a long way from school, grandchildren may mean that they are closer to education than they have been for some years.
4. Recruiting new people into the group is a continual process.

   After the initial burst, recruitment of people into the group is often given a low priority, and the group's membership starts a steady decline. Continuous promotion of activities, opportunities, and needs is vital for long-term growth.

Fundraising

5. Fundraising must also be continuous.

Two suggestions:

(a) give specific responsibility for fundraising to a committee member to ensure it does not get lost amongst other priorities.

(b) include donation slips/covenant forms within all your main information mailings.

6. The more personal a fundraising approach, the better:

Method	Effectiveness
Letter	✓
Telephone Call	✓✓
Face to face meeting	✓✓✓

7. The more specific, the better:

Approach	Effectiveness
'We would like money'	✓
'We would like money for a computer'	✓✓
'We would like money for a computer that will enable us to computerise our database so that we can keep our supporters better informed, whilst also freeing up more time for schools work'	✓✓✓

8. The more immediate to the potential supporter, the better:

Approach	Effectiveness
'We are invited to speak at various schools'	✓
'We are invited to speak at schools in your local area'	✓✓
'We are invited to speak at Sometown School, which your children attend'	✓✓✓

Further information

If you would like to know how to form your group into a charity, thereby benefiting from tax benefits that could increase the amount of money you receive from supporters, more information is included in Appendix IV.

If you are an individual wanting to find out if there is an

existing group for schools near you, Part 3 has contact details of the School Ministry Network, which can put you in contact with any groups and full-time schools workers in your area.

Part Two

Ten Assembly Scripts

Find out what others do, then do your own thing...

A professional writer once said that 'bad writers plagiarise, good writers steal', and I think the same could be said of those who lead assemblies. 'Off-the-shelf' scripts are perhaps most useful as starting points for individuals to come up with their own material, which reflects their own style. Please feel free to 'steal' from the assemblies in this section and then use the ideas in your own way.

These scripts tend to be on the short side; this gives you the opportunity to bring in personal experience and relevant anecdotes. The props that are suggested are usually readily available and full-page illustrations have been included at the end of some assemblies for photocopying or using as OHP transparencies. However, remember that it may take time to get together everything you need – these are not designed to be 'instant assemblies'.

Please read on...

John 13:14 – Jesus' humility

Audience:
Secondary school pupils

Learning objective:
Christians believe that Jesus showed humility.

Biblical basis:
John 13:14 '...I, your Lord and Teacher, have washed your feet...'
Matthew 11:29 '...I am gentle and humble in heart.'
Mark 10:45 'For even the Son of Man did not come to be served, but to serve, and to give his life as a ransom for many.'

Summary:
Step 1: Important people usually have status symbols.
Step 2: In contrast, Jesus was humble.
Step 3: Moreover, Jesus served his followers.

Number of speakers:
Four – main presenter, 'older disciple', 'younger disciple', 'Jesus'.

Equipment:
For the opening exercise:
● Twelve large cards (perhaps about B4 size: 36cm x 30cm) with the following clearly written on:
'Rolls Royce'; 'Mercedes'; 'Porsche'; 'Ford Mondeo'; 'Lada';

'3-wheel car'
'The Queen'; 'Middle-aged businessman'; 'Young film star';
'Teacher'; 'Teenager/student'; 'Pensioner'

● Three cards need to have a word on the reverse side:

'Rolls Royce'	→	'Chariot'
'Porsche'	→	'War horse'
One of the cheaper cars	→	'Donkey'

For the drama:
● A basin (a washing up bowl will do), water, small towel, and a wet cloth.

Script

(In advance, pin up the cards bearing car names near where you are to speak from. There should be space for other cards to be pinned next to them. The order of the 'car cards' should be: Rolls Royce; Mercedes; Porsche; Ford Mondeo; Lada; 3-wheel car.)

Introduction
In today's assembly we're going to be thinking about the character of Jesus; we'll do this by looking at what important people are usually like, and then comparing them to Jesus.
(ask for a volunteer and hand him or her the cards with types of people on them)

Step 1: Important people usually have status symbols.
Up here are six cards with makes of cars on them. My volunteer has six cards with types of people on them. What I would like her to do is to match the people with the cars they are most likely to drive. Go!

(On completion, draw out the fact that the people with higher status are generally matched with the prestige cars, whilst others don't have status symbols. Thank the volunteer)

Step 2: In contrast, Jesus was humble.

Now let me take you back 2,000 years. There weren't any cars then, but there were still status-symbols for people who were considered to be 'important'. The equivalent of Rolls Royce *(point to the top of the list of cars)* were expensive chariots *(turn over a 'Rolls Royce' card to show the word 'chariot')*.

The equivalent of a Porsche might have been a war-horse *(turn over the 'Porsche' card)*.

About 2,000 years ago, a few days before the Jewish feast of Passover, the word went out around Jerusalem that Jesus was going to be coming to the city. There was tremendous excitement, because Jesus was claiming great things about himself, and had done many miracles that seemed to show that he came from God. As the time ticked away towards Passover, you can imagine some of the gossip there might have been. 'Jesus is coming; he'll try to really impress everybody. Is he going to come in a limousine-chariot? Or is he perhaps going to opt for the classic appeal of a war-horse?'

It must have been a great shock when Jesus actually made his triumphal entry into Jerusalem .... riding a donkey. This was the equivalent of a cheap car that isn't much of a status symbol at all *(turn over one of the car cards to reveal the word 'donkey').*

People must have wondered what he was on. What sort of great leader comes riding in on a donkey? There were really only two conclusions. Either Jesus was not actually a great leader at all, or else he was a great leader, but in a different way to what everyone was used to.

Jesus was different. Jesus was humble. And this wasn't just seen in the transport he used. Here's some drama:

Step 3: Moreover, Jesus served his followers.

Two 'disciples' recline on chairs. They are wearing sports gear, training shoes, and thick white, dirty socks.

OLDER DISCIPLE: *(lounging in chair)*
What a long hot day it's been! We've been walking around
Jerusalem for hours. Thank goodness Jesus has arranged our
supper. Phew! I'm covered in sweat.
(wipes forehead, then scratches both armpits)

YOUNGER DISCIPLE:
Me too – Jerusalem's much too hot for me. It's hard work
following Jesus.
*(wipes a cloth over his forehead – the cloth should already be
wet – and then wrings out the water)*

OLDER DISCIPLE:
Well, we'll soon be able to have supper. I've already washed my
hands – you've just got to wash my feet *(starts to take off shoes)*.

YOUNGER DISCIPLE:
What do you mean: I've just got to wash your feet? I don't want
to do that.

OLDER DISCIPLE:
I'm older than you, so you should serve me *(removes shoe)*.

YOUNGER DISCIPLE:
But your feet ... *(puts nose close to sock)* ...smell. Ugh!

OLDER DISCIPLE:
Don't try and get out of it. You're the youngest and lowest. *(lifts leg and sticks the sock near the younger disciple's face)*. It's your job.

YOUNGER DISCIPLE:
Awww .... Look, here comes Jesus.

OLDER DISCIPLE: *(stands up)*
Good evening Teacher. Jesus, you are the Lord, tell our young upstart here that he has to serve you and me, and wash our feet.

JESUS:
Sit down. *(Older disciple sits down)*
Take off your socks. *(Older disciple does this, unwillingly)*

YOUNGER DISCIPLE: *(as the smell reaches him and his nose wrinkles in distaste)*
Ugh! That is a disgusting smell.

(Jesus reaches over to the basin and starts to wash the older disciple's feet).

OLDER DISCIPLE:
Jesus, surely you're not going to wash my feet – you're the Lord! *(gestures with his hands helplessly – then sits back realising he can do nothing but let Jesus wash and dry his feet)*
…Well, I must say I feel a bit foolish now…

JESUS: *(facing towards the audience, although ostensibly talking to the disciples)*
Do you understand what I have just done to you?

* * *

MAIN PRESENTER: Do you understand what Jesus was doing? The Bible tells us that Jesus said to his followers *(reads from a Good News Version)*: 'I, your Lord and Teacher, have just washed your feet. You, then, should wash one another's feet. I have set an example for you, so that you'll do just what I've done for you.'[1]

In serving others, Jesus *(touch 'Jesus')* was very different from the self-seeking behaviour of some of his followers *(touch the 'older disciple')*.

How would we apply Jesus' example to our own lives? It might not be a case of washing people's feet, but it might mean washing dishes at home, and thinking about what we can do for those around us in other ways.

(Optional)
I would like to finish by asking you to be silent for twenty seconds and think about two things that you might do for your family and friends...

Optional prayer:
Heavenly Father,
Please make us to be more like Jesus
Please help us to be humble, and to serve others.
Amen.

Song suggestion:
An appropriate song to be sung as a solo would be *From heaven you came* (Graham Kendrick)

> From heaven you came, helpless babe,
> Entered our world, your glory veiled;
> Not to be served but to serve,
> And give your life that we might live.
>
> *This is our God, the Servant King,*
> *He calls us now to follow him,*
> *To bring our lives as a daily offering*
> *Of worship to the Servant King.*

There in the garden of tears,
My heavy load he chose to bear;
His heart with sorrow was torn,
'Yet not My will but yours' he said.

This is our God...

Come see his hands and his feet,
The scars that speak of sacrifice,
Hands that flung stars into space
To cruel nails surrendered.

This is our God...

So let us learn how to serve,
And in our lives enthrone him;
Each other's needs to prefer,
For it is Christ we're serving.

This is our God...

Options:
To reduce time
● Discard the opening activity
● Discard the first two steps entirely and just keep the drama.

To increase time
● Think of more ways in which young people could apply the message of the assembly practically

Comments:
● If there is no one to assist with the drama, it could be paraphrased.

Luke 10:25-37 – Active response

Audience:
Secondary school pupils

Learning objective:
Christians believe that people should actively respond to those in need.

Biblical Basis:
Luke 10:34 – 'He *(the Samaritan)* went to him and bandaged his wounds'

Summary:
Step 1: Some people think that they're good enough for God because they don't do bad things.
Step 2: However, God wants us actively to do good.

Number of presenters:
Two

Equipment:
● Exam paper (perhaps an old one, borrowed from the school);
● A long ruler – preferably a metre ruler
● A pillow or cushion
● A pillowcase with the face of an unhappy man drawn on it
● Pretend money
● An old alarm clock (optional)
● A plaster bandage

- Glasses of water (preferably pint glasses)
- Items of clothing to denote respectability (such as a tie) and something less respectable (such as a baseball cap that could be worn backwards).

Script

There is a table on one end of the stage, with a few pint-glasses full of water on it to represent the inn.

Step 1: Some people think that they're good enough for God because they don't do bad things.

MAIN PRESENTER:
Something that you'll all know about are exams. *(Holds up exam paper and looks at it)* In the exam paper that I have here, the passmark was 50%. If you could imagine that this ruler gives the scale of marks *(holds a ruler vertically)* then if you got less than 50% *(points to below half way point on the ruler)*, you'd be under the passmark and fail, but as long as you got more than 50% *(points to above the half-way point on the ruler)* you'd be good enough to pass.

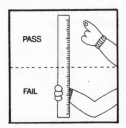

Some people think that in life, a bit like in exams, there is a passmark which is set by God. Imagine that this is the passmark they are thinking of *(point to half-way point on the ruler)*: they might say that you could be below the passmark *(point to below half-way)* if you murder somebody or if you are like Hitler or something really awful. But so long as you avoid doing really bad things, you'd be good enough to pass *(point to above half-way)*; God would have to be pleased with you.

Step 2: However, God wants us actively to do good.
That's not something that Jesus taught *(get rid of the ruler)*, so now I want to look at what Jesus did say. We're going to retell a 'story with a message' – a parable – that Jesus told.[1]

(Ask for a volunteer – ideally he or she will have been picked in advance and will know what is expected)

The volunteer represents somebody who – I don't know whether you'll be able to do this – is a thug. Do you think you can manage that? *(ask her to stand near the middle of the stage)*

An important character in the story is this man *(holds up pillow, with a drawing of a man on the pillowcase)*. One day, this man is walking along a mountainous road on his way to the city of Jericho *(props the pillow on centre of the stage)*. It's a dangerous area, known for attacks by bandits. The man walks along carefully, looking out for any trouble. Suddenly a brutal, fearsome thug jumps out and beats him up *(The 'thug' is encouraged to beat up the pillow and stand on it. Then she should be asked to sit back down in her place)*.

The victim is lying half-dead on the road. But it so happened that a little later a respectable man – a priest – comes along the same road *(the second presenter – dressed in appropriately respectable clothes – comes close to the 'victim').*

The priest was the sort of person who knows about religion, and he's not a murderer or a thief or anything like that. He's the sort of person who might think that he's 'good enough' as far as God is concerned.

He sees the victim, lying in agony on the path, and... he doesn't want to take the risk of doing anything to help. He doesn't want to spend his time showing love to a stranger in need... *('Priest' takes an alarm clock out of his pocket, shakes his head, and then puts it securely back)* and he doesn't want to risk his money *('Priest' takes money out of his pocket, and then puts it securely back)*. He passes by on the other side.

A short time later a different person comes along. This person is also respectable *(the second presenter rapidly changes his or her appearance – for example, puts on a tie)*. Like the first one, he thinks he's living a pretty good life, but when it comes to positively helping someone he has never met, well... he might do...

('Levite' goes over and looks at the victim, but then shakes his head and says 'He's not one of us'. *He then resumes his stately progress).*

The poor victim is still in agony here on the path. He's had a bad kicking from the fearsome thug. He needs help. Oh, here comes a man from Samaria – people of other nationalities look down on the inhabitants of Samaria.

(The second presenter changes again – for example, removes tie and puts on baseball hat backwards; saunters to the centre of the stage)

'SAMARITAN': *(taking care to talk in the direction of the audience throughout)* Oh, look at this poor person *(picks up pillow)*. I must do something to help him. Of course it's a bit dangerous here... but I can't just leave him – I'll take him to the nearest inn *(picks up pillow, puts a bandage on it, and then carries it carefully over to the 'inn')*.

Hello landlord *(spoken to the main presenter who has moved to stand behind the table with the pint-glasses)*. Could you look after this poor man? Here's some money *(counts out all his money)*. Take care of him and when I come back this way, I'll pay you whatever else you spend on him.

MAIN PRESENTER: *(moving away from the 'inn')* That's how the story ends, and when he had finished telling it, Jesus said: 'go and do the same'.[2]

I wonder what our reaction is to that story?

Don't you think that it's true that some people think that they live 'good' lives, yet they don't seem to go out of their way to help other people in need, particularly if they are not part of their group? Such people might not do bad things, but they pass by on the other side when there's a chance to do good things.

One of the reasons why this story of Jesus is challenging is because it teaches that it's not good enough just to avoid harming others; instead, it teaches that we should actively respond to others in need, like the Samaritan did.

So for example... *(add applications as appropriate to pupils' situations, if desired)*

Optional prayer:
Heavenly Father,
Thank you for giving us a model of how to live.
It's not always easy to live up to that model.
So please help us, through Jesus, to be more like the Good Samaritan.
Amen

Song suggestions:
Give me oil in my lamp (traditional) *Junior Praise* No 50 – especially the third verse.

Options:
To reduce time
● Cut out the landlord – this part of the story can be paraphrased by the main presenter.

To increase time
● Step 3 could be developed by introducing the idea that, as we

all fail at some point to live up to the model shown by the Good Samaritan, we need help from God. Christians believe this help is provided by Jesus. (Note: this is hinted at in the prayer). This could lead into an account of how the presenter or someone not present realised their need for a Saviour, and how Jesus met this need.

Comments:

● The Good Samaritan has a number of different points – this is by no means the only message that can be drawn out of it.

Luke 16:19-31 –
The rich man and Lazarus

Audience:
Secondary school pupils

Learning objective:
Christians believe that being right with God is more important than being rich.

Biblical basis:
Luke 16:22 '...the beggar died and the angels carried him to Abraham's side. The rich man also died and was buried. In hell, where he was in torment, he looked up and saw Abraham far away...'

Summary:
Step 1: Some people love money.
Step 2: However, Christians believe that being right with God is more important than being rich.

Number of speakers:
One main presenter with four non-speaking assistants:

Main presenter	–	Narrator
Assistant 1	–	'Abraham'
Assistant 2	–	'Rich man'
Assistant 3	–	'Lazarus'
Assistant 4	–	'Angel'

Alternative: The part of the 'angel' could be carried out by the main presenter if necessary, so that only three assistants are needed.

Suggestion: The non-speaking assistants might for example be members of the school's Christian Union.

Equipment:

For rich man:
- Small chocolate bar
- 'Cool' sunglasses

For poor man:
- An outer-garment that makes him look poor – for example, old overalls.

General:
- Large packet of chocolate bars
- Eight black bin liners
- Four white bin liners
- Chairs
- A Bible (Good News version)
- A box (an old cereal packet would do) covered in paper with the word 'Life' written on it in large letters
- Loose change
- Ice cubes (if possible)
- A rock

Comments:

1. The content of this assembly should definitely be discussed with teachers in advance, as it specifically mentions death and afterlife. I have used it for a group that I know fairly well; I probably wouldn't use it as the first assembly that I led at a school.
2. This is best done on a stage so that everyone can see what is happening. If there is no stage, the characters will need to stand so that they can be seen clearly.
3. The main presenter needs to pause during the reading of the story to allow miming to take place as indicated in the script. To make the reading more dramatic, use expression as appropriate.

4. The assistants need to have rehearsed their miming roles beforehand.

Script

(To begin with the main presenter stands alone at the front beside a table. There is a row of three chairs on the left of the presentation area and a row of four chairs on the right. The white bin liners are laid out in a line just in front of the chairs on the right. The black bin bags are spread out to form an area of plastic several feet further away from those chairs. The assistants sit in the front row, ready to come forward on their cue.

Today's assembly is about what's really important in life.

Step 1: Some people love money
For some people, everything in their lives seems to rest on money *(take change out of trouser pocket or purse, put it in piles on the table, and set the 'Life' box on it).*

They believe their happiness and security are based on their money and their savings and all the different things they own. For example, they might think they'd be completely happy if only they had the best trainers about, or the trendiest clothes, or the latest computer games.[1]

There's a group of people just like this in the Bible,[2] and they were told a story[3] by Jesus that we're going to retell today.

There are four characters in this story Jesus told. The first one is a rich man *('rich man' comes to the front)* whose life rested on how much money he had *(point to 'Life' box)*.

He's expensively dressed, wearing all the latest gear. He's got a wonderful house and eats the finest food *('rich man' lounges on the row of seats on the left)*.

The second character is a poor man called Lazarus *('Lazarus' comes forward)*. He lives in the street outside the rich man's house *('Lazarus' kneels by the chairs on the left)*.

The third character is Abraham. He is mentioned a lot in the first book of the Bible. He died a long time ago. Abraham was God's friend, and so now that he has died he is in a good place *('Abraham' sits on the chairs on the right)*.

The final character is an angel.

Step 2: Christians believe that being right with God is more important than being rich.

(This script is based on the Good News Bible.)

Once there was a rich man who dressed in the most expensive clothes and lived in luxury every day (*'rich man' stretches himself and indulgently starts to eat small chocolate bar*).

There was also a poor man named Lazarus. He was covered with sores. He used to be brought to the rich man's door, hoping to eat the bits of food that fell from the rich man's table... (*'Lazarus' tries in vain to attract 'rich man's' attention to have some of the chocolate bar*)

The poor man died (*'Lazarus' keels over*) and was carried by the angels to sit beside Abraham at the feast in heaven (*'Angel' drags 'Lazarus' a short way towards the chairs on the right, then gets him to get up and sit on the chairs alongside 'Abraham'. 'Abraham' produces a whole packet of chocolate bars, and 'Lazarus' starts to open one*).

The rich man also died (*'rich man' takes off dark glasses, looks quizzical, then dies dramatically*) ...and he was buried (*'rich man' rolls gently onto the floor. 'Angel' drags him a short way, then gets him to go over to stand on the black binliners. 'Rich man' sinks to his knees in despair when he gets there*).

In Hades[4] he was in great pain *(pause)*. The rich man looked up and saw Abraham, far away, with Lazarus at his side. So he called out:

'Father Abraham! Take pity on me... (*'rich man' reaches out his hands beseechingly towards 'Abraham'*)

… and send Lazarus to dip his finger in some water and cool my tongue, because I am in great pain in this fire.'

But Abraham said: 'Remember, my son, that in your lifetime you were given all the good things *('Abraham' gestures towards the chairs where the 'rich man' once lounged)*, while Lazarus got all the bad things. But now he is enjoying himself here *('Abraham' puts his arm on 'Lazarus'' shoulder)*, while you are in pain.

Besides all that, there is a deep pit lying between us *('Abraham' points down)*, so that those who want to cross over from here to you cannot do so, nor can anyone cross over to us from where you are.'

The rich man said: 'Then I beg you, father Abraham, *('rich man', kneeling, spreads out his arms in supplication)* send Lazarus to my father's house, where I have five brothers. Let him go and warn them so that they, at least, will not come to this place of pain.'

Abraham said: 'Your brothers have Moses and the prophets to warn them; your brothers should listen to what they say.'

The rich man answered: 'That is not enough, father Abraham! But if someone were to rise from death and go to them, then they would turn from their sins.'

But Abraham said: 'If they will not listen to Moses and the Prophets, they will not be convinced *(read the last part of the sentence slower)* even if someone were to rise from death'. *(Pause).*

That's the end of Jesus' story. *('Characters' sit down where they are).*

Let's think back to the people to whom Jesus was telling that story. I wonder what their reaction would have been? Their lives had money as the foundations *(point to 'Life' box)*, and after this story which shows what happened to the rich man, I wonder if they were beginning to think that money was actually a poor sort of foundation. Jesus' story would seem to suggest that money, instead of being durable and solid, is actually more like ice *(replace coins with a few ice blocks, and briefly hold the 'Life' box on top of them).*

Ice is not very stable, and not very good in the long term. In the story, the rich man's money did not help him when it mattered.

Christians believe that being right with God, like Lazarus was *(point to 'Lazarus')*, is much more important than having lots of money. The Bible sometimes talk of God as a Rock *(put rock on table)*, and Christians believe people should base their lives on reliable rock *(put 'Life' box on it)*, rather than on money.

Just as the story was challenging for the people to whom Jesus was originally talking, it's still challenging for us now – where are our priorities? Do they take into account the long term?

Optional prayer:
Heavenly Father,
Please help us to get our priorities right.
Please help us to understand what's really important in life.
Amen.

Song suggestions:
Seek ye first the Kingdom of God (Karen Lafferty) *Junior Praise* No 215

Options:
To shorten time:
It is difficult to shorten this, and therefore it would be a good idea to agree in advance with teachers how much time will be needed.

To increase time:
Further encouragements to think through priorities in life,
perhaps using your own experience to say that, in all the things
you've done in the life, deciding to become a Christian was the
most crucial.

Genesis 1:1 – God as creator

Audience:
Secondary school (lower age-groups)

Learning objective:
Christians believe that God made the world and everything in it.

Biblical basis:
Genesis 1:1 'In the beginning God created the heavens and the earth...'[1]
Acts 17:24 'God, who made the world and everything in it, is Lord of heaven and earth ...'[2]
Romans 1: 20 'Ever since God created the world, his invisible qualities, both his eternal power and his divine nature, have been clearly seen; they are perceived in the things that God has made.'

Summary:
Step 1: Man-made things are amazing, but creation is even more amazing.
Step 2: Christians believe that a creator God is responsible for such amazing things.

Numbers of speakers: One

Equipment:
● Three boxes, each covered with coloured paper. One should contain a smoke alarm, the second a battery-operated torch, and the third a Venus fly-catcher plant

117

- A see-through tray (eg made of clear plastic) filled with electrical odds and ends such as plugs and fuses
- A large card with a picture of a technical-looking man on it, sub-titled 'engineer'
- A large card with the word 'God' on it
- Something to represent the world – for example a globe, or a drawing of the world map stuck onto the reverse side of the smoke alarm

Comments:
- This basic Christian message may not be appropriate for schools with a tradition of Christian assemblies.
- It might be easiest to stand behind a table so that the props are within easy reach.

Script

Step 1: Man-made things are amazing, but creation is even more amazing.
(Ask for two volunteers)
There's a mystery object in each of the three boxes on the centre table. I'm going to read out clues about them. I would like my volunteers to call out guesses of what they are.

The first one is a **fairly amazing** thing that is man-made, is in most houses, helps to protect the house and people in it, makes a loud bleeping noise when activated, is recommended by the fire brigade ... a smoke alarm *(open box to show what it is)*.

The second is also a **fairly amazing** thing. It's man-made, it is very useful for part of a twenty-four hour period, though it's not useful all the time. It's easy to carry about. It has a bulb... a torch *(open box to show what it is)*.

The third mystery object is an **incredibly amazing** thing. It is not man-made, it has a touch-sensitive mechanism that means it can trap things that move quickly, it is very efficient at using the energy it gets out of sunlight... it's a Venus fly-trap – a plant which catches flies *(open box to show it)*.

(Thank volunteers and send them back to their seats)

The things which are man-made *(point to the smoke alarm and torch)* are amazing. But natural things around us – like this Venus flytrap – can be even more amazing. How did things as amazing as this come about?

Step 2: Christians believe that a creator God is responsible for such amazing things.

Think about the smoke alarm for a moment *(hold it up)*; it didn't come about by chance. It wasn't as if there was a whole load of components sitting about *(lift up tray full of miscellaneous electrical components)*,

and then one day there was a freak accident *(shake the tray)* and they suddenly formed themselves into a complete smoke alarm.

The smoke alarm was actually the result of careful planning by an engineer *(hold up card showing a technical person whilst continuing to hold the smoke alarm in the other. Then put them both back onto the table).*

In a similar way Christians believe that the world around us *(hold up a representation of the world)...*

...was planned and made by God *(in the other hand, hold up a card with the word 'God' on it)*

Some of the very first words of the Bible are:[3]
    'In the beginning God created the heavens and the earth...'

(put the props in your hands back onto the table)

Christians believe that, because God made the natural world around us, then looking at it and thinking about it can show us something of God, even though God himself can't be seen.

Think for a moment about this torch *(pick up the torch)*. It's fairly easy to explain how this torch works. We can see that there's a bulb *(show bulb)* and there's a battery that provides the power *(hold up a battery)*.

As well as seeing *how* it works, we also need to ask *why* it works. The reason why this torch comes on is that... somebody wants it to. Maybe it's dark and I would like to have light, so I decide to switch it on *(switch the torch on, then off again)*.

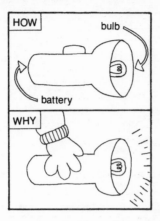

Let's now imagine this torch represents the world in which we live. We can explain *how* the world works – we know a lot about science *(represented by the bulb)* and technology *(represented by the battery)*.

But explaining how doesn't explain why the world was made. *Why* did it come about in the first place? Christians believe that we need to look to an incredibly powerful God *(switch on the torch)*. The Bible tells us that it was God who first said 'Let there be light'.[4]

One of the followers of Jesus[5] summed it up something like this:

'The basic reality of God is plain enough. Open your eyes and there it is! By taking a long and thoughtful look at what God has created, people have always been able to see what their eyes as such can't see: eternal power, for instance, and the mystery of his divine being.'[6]

So Christians believe that God made the world and everything in it[7] – what do you think? I'd like to encourage you to think about your own views.

Optional prayer:

Heavenly Father,
Thank you for creating the world, and creating us.
Amen.

Song suggestions:
All things bright and beautiful (Cecil F Alexander) *Junior Praise* No 6
Think of a world without any flowers (Doreen Newport) *Junior Praise* No 254

Options:
To reduce time
● Reveal what is in the boxes immediately after reading out the clues.
● Leave out the illustration which uses the torch.

To increase time
● Have more mystery objects, and make it a competition between the two volunteers to see who can guess more of them.
● Demonstrate how the Venus fly-plant reacts to moving objects by touching its triggers.

Other options
● Instead of asking for volunteers at the beginning, explain that anyone can put up their hand if they have guessed the answer, and that the main speaker will pick on people to answer. A variation of this would be to divide the pupils into two teams – for example, those sitting on the left of the central aisle form one team, and those sitting on the right form another one.

engineer

Matthew 11:28 – Rest from life's burdens

Audience:
Secondary school pupils

Learning objective:
Christians believe that Jesus can give people rest from life's burdens.

Biblical basis:
Matthew 11:28 'Come to me, all you who are weary and burdened, and I will give you rest. Take my yoke upon you and learn from me, for I am gentle and humble in heart, and you will find rest for your souls. For my yoke is easy and my burden is light'.[1]

Summary:
Step 1: Life can have burdens
Step 2: Christians believe that Jesus can give people rest from life's burdens.

Number of speakers:
Two. (Alternatively, one speaker and one non-speaking assistant)

Equipment:
- 3 bags (strong carrier bags would do). One bag has the words 'Life's Burdens' on it – this could be on a sheet of paper taped to the front.
- Weights to put in the bags – for example, books, stones…

- Heavy objects such as books covered with paper and with the following words on them:- 'Worry', 'Lonely', and 'Guilt'.
- Another six light objects covered with paper and with the word 'Guilt' on them.
- *Optional* – a nautical/pirate outfit for the second presenter.
- *Optional* – an OHP with slides as illustrated later.

Script

Step 1: Life can have burdens

Explain that to start with there is going to be a competition of strength. Two volunteers are each given a bag containing weights such as heavy books. They have to hold the bags with arms stretched out in front of them, at shoulder height. The aim is to hold this position for as long as possible. Ensure that the load is heavy enough so that the contest only lasts a minute – add more weight depending on the age-group of pupils. Encourage the volunteers as appropriate – perhaps a running commentary on how uncomfortable they are looking, whether their arms are starting to shake, and so on. Ensure that their arms are kept straight and at shoulder height – if a volunteer

drops their arms below the horizontal, then he or she has lost.

Reward the winner (a chocolate bar to replace lost energy?) and the loser (with the same). Send them back to their places.

Sometimes people feel that they're carrying loads; not physical ones, as in the competition, but in their hearts. You may know the expression 'there's a weight on my shoulders' or maybe you've heard people talk about 'life's burdens'. Maybe they feel a bit like this... *(hold up the bag with 'Life's Burdens' on it).*

Let's have a look at what those burdens might be... *(Open bag and pull out the weights in it – they might for example be books covered in brown paper, appropriately labeled).*

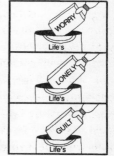

'Worry' – sometimes people are anxious about life. It might be exams that make them anxious, or something at home.

'Loneliness' – some people do get lonely, and this can be hard to bear sometimes.

'Guilt' – some people feel bad about

things they've done that they know were wrong, and they carry guilt about with them.

I'd like to tell you a story about a man who carried a great weight in his life. Imagine that we're going back 200 years in time. Let me introduce you to... *(second presenter moves forward. Ideally he would have a nautical appearance, like a pirate)*

...John Newton. John Newton is a deeply unpleasant man. He trades in something awful – not drugs, but slaves. In the eighteenth century John Newton used to take slaves across the Atlantic Ocean in a small ship so that they could be sold to big slave-owners – at least the ones who survived the appalling conditions on John Newton's ships could be sold.

Each time that he did these awful things, John Newton had a bigger and bigger weight of guilt. *(Main presenter hands the bag with 'Life's Burdens' written on it over to 'John Newton', who holds it out like the volunteers did earlier. The main presenter then puts five or six weights with the word 'Guilt' written on them into the bag, explaining that each slave-trip increased his guilt. Note that 'John Newton' needs to be able to hold the*

weight of the bag easily; the 'weights' could be empty boxes covered with brown paper?)

Step 2: Christians believe that Jesus can give people rest from life's burdens.

One day a storm hit John Newton's ship during one of his voyages. A strong gale whipped up the water and soon waves were crashing over the vessel.

With water pouring all over him and with the wind wailing about him, he thought he was going to die. And as he faced death, he saw as never before what a weight of guilt he was carrying (*'John Newton' mimes strain of holding the bag*).

At that moment, he turned to Jesus Christ. Jesus says in the Bible: 'Come to me, all of you who are tired from carrying heavy loads, and I will give you rest.'[2]

John Newton prayed to Jesus in the midst of the storm, feeling completely weighed down by his past life, and he felt that Jesus was coming to the rescue *(main presenter supports the bottom of the bag, taking the weight of it.*

As this is done, he or she could repeat: 'Jesus said: "Come to me, all of you who are tired from carrying heavy loads, and I will give you rest". *Then the main presenter takes the bag completely, and puts it on the floor).*

There is a sequel to this story. John Newton survived the storm, but afterwards he was a changed man. He no longer worked as a slave-trader; instead, he put a lot of effort into campaigning against slavery. His efforts were one of the reasons why several years later the British Parliament passed an Act abolishing the slave-trade.

The change that had come over him led some people to ridicule him, and they began to hate him because of his new determination to do the right thing. But for John Newton, the difficulties of his new life were small compared to the joy he had now that the weight of guilt had been lifted from him by Jesus. John Newton wrote some words about the undeserved love, or 'grace' that he had experienced from Jesus who had taken away the burdens of his life.

('John Newton' reads...)

> *Amazing grace – how sweet the sound –*
> *That saved a wretch like me!*
> *I once was lost, but now am found;*
> *Was blind, but now I see.*

> *God's grace first taught my heart to fear,*
> *His grace my fears relieved;*
> *How precious did that grace appear*
> *The hour I first believed!*

Christians believe that the 'grace' or undeserved love that John Newton talked about is still being given out by Jesus. John Newton's life was completely transformed during one storm; for others, the change is more gradual.

But whether sudden or gradual, Christians believe that Jesus is still coming to people's rescue, and that he's still giving rest to people tired from carrying the heavy loads of life.

Optional prayer:
Heavenly Father,
Thank you for your love for us.
Thank you through Jesus Christ that we can have rest from
carrying heavy loads.
Amen

Songs:
Amazing Grace by John Newton (perhaps sung as a solo?)
God is so good (composer unknown) *Junior Praise* No 53

Options:
To reduce time
● To shorten the initial competition, put extra weights in the
bags to begin with, or else ask volunteers to use one arm only.
● Cut out the reading of verses from *Amazing Grace*.

To increase time
● Lengthen the initial competition by having more contestants.
● Read more verses of 'Amazing Grace'. Other verses are:-

> *Through every danger, trial and snare*
> *I have already come;*
> *His grace has brought me safe thus far,*
> *And grace will lead me home.*

> *The Lord has promised good to me,*
> *His word my hope secures;*
> *My shield and stronghold he shall be*
> *As long as life endures.*

And when this earthly life is past,
And mortal cares shall cease,
I shall possess with Christ at last
Eternal joy and peace.

J. Newton (1725–1807)

● Illustrate the weights of 'anxiety', 'loneliness', and 'guilt' with examples relevant to the pupils. For example, 'anxiety' might be illustrated by the manager of the local football club if it is facing relegation.

Selling
Slaves

John 1:18 – How can we know God?

Audience:
6th form.

Learning objective:
Christians believe that Jesus has made God known.

Biblical basis:
John 1:18 – "No-one has ever seen God. The only Son, who is the same as God and is at the Father's side, he has made him known"[1]

Summary:
Introduction
Step 1: We have to work out what we believe in.
Step 2: Some things are easy to believe in because of clear evidence.
Step 3: God can be hard to believe in because we can't see him.
Step 4: However, Christians believe Jesus has made God known.
Application: When people believe in God, their lives have to change.

Number of speakers:
One

Equipment:
Either
● OHP slides – see later.

Or

● A large cardboard box, a model of a person (for example an 'Action Man' toy man, a doll, or a cut-out man), a lamp (an extension lead might be necessary), a chocolate bar.

Comments:

This outline is based on an assembly taken by Ian Garrett. It was originally written as a 'Christmas' assembly for the 6th form at a school with a tradition of distinctively Christian assemblies. He used OHP slides (given at the end of this outline); the OHP was operated by an assistant to minimise distraction to the speaker. The version given here uses physical props rather than OHPs.

Script

Introduction

Today I want to examine one important issue: how can we know about God? To help us look at that, I've brought along a box *(place it on its side on a table in the centre of the presentation area)* and a model person *(stand the man inside the box).*

Step 1: We have to work out what we believe in.

I'd like you to imagine that the person is you or me. And the box is your life or mine. So it's got a beginning – the left hand end of the box. It's going to have an end – the right hand side *(point to the two sides as appropriate).* And in the middle, all of us have got to try to sort out what we're going to do with the time we've been given. We're going to have to work out for ourselves what we think matters in life – apart from obvious things like who wins the Premiership this season. We're going to have to work out what we believe in.

Step 2: Some things are easy to believe in because of indisputable evidence.

Now some things are really easy to believe in. Chocolate, for example *(hold up a bar of chocolate).* I've never had a problem believing in chocolate. I doubt you have. The thing about chocolate is that you can see it – and taste it. You know it's there. *(Put the bar into the box).*

But we also believe in things we can't see. I bet if I asked for a show of hands, you'd all say you believe in oxygen. But I'm sure you've never seen it. You can't – at least not directly. But even though you can't see it in the way you can see chocolate *(point to the bar in the box)*, you can be sure it's there *(point to the air in the box).*

Step 3: God can be hard to believe in because we can't see him.

But what about God? Is he really there? On Sunday lots of people go to church, and sing about God and pray to God and talk to God. But are they just guessing? The trouble is: we can't see him.

The first man to orbit the earth was called Yuri Gagarin. He was an atheist, and a bit cynical. So when he'd done the orbit, he radioed back to earth: 'Well I've been all the way round, and I haven't seen God'. That's the attitude of a lot of people. Can't see him, so presumably he isn't there.

Step 4: However, Christians believe Jesus has made God known.

Well, Christians are sure that God is there. We believe that God is ruling above us – let's show that by a lamp *(put a lamp on top of the box, and switch it on).* He rules even though we can't actually see out of our box.

The question is: how can we say that? How can we be sure that God is there?

The answer is in a verse out of John's Gospel – one of the four books in the Bible about the events of Jesus' life. It's basically a verse about Christmas.

The first half of the verse goes like this: 'No one has ever seen God.' That bit's pretty easy to agree with, I reckon. 'No one has ever seen God but...

...the only Son, who is the same as God and is at the Father's side, he has made him known'   .

Just imagine for a moment that God really is there. And that he wanted us to be aware of that – and to know him. And just imagine that he took the initiative: he sent his own Son from his side (up on top of the box) to our side (in the box). So we could actually see him, and be sure he's there, and know what he wants for our lives. *(Rotate the lamp so that its light shines directly down into the interior of the box, whilst keeping the base of the lamp on the top of the box).*

Christians say that you don't have to imagine that. We believe that the facts show that it actually happened. It happened when Jesus was born in Bethlehem on the first Christmas.

Application: When people believe in God, their lives have to change.

Now if this is true, what difference does it make? Well, those people who do think it's true can't honestly be atheists or agnostics any more. Atheists say 'there's definitely no God', and agnostics say 'you can never know whether there is a God or not'. But people can't say those things if they believe that Jesus came from God and has made God known.

From where I stand as a Christian speaker, it seems to me that if I think that Jesus *has* made God known, then there are really only two things I can end up saying to God. Either I say to God, 'I know you're there, but I don't want you interfering with the way I run my life'. Or I say, 'I know you're there, and I want to get to know you and how life is supposed to work.'

The question that we're then left with is: 'which of these two things do I think I'm saying to God right now?' And, 'Which one of these two things do I *want* to be saying to God?'

Perhaps, as you go away from here, some of you might want to think about those questions.

Optional prayer:
God our Heavenly Father,
Thank you that we can know you through Jesus your only Son.
Amen

Illustrations for OHP slides are given on the next three pages. A crown is used to visualise God rather than a lamp.

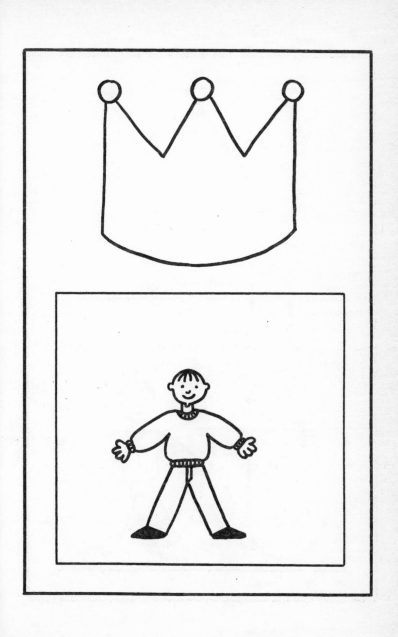

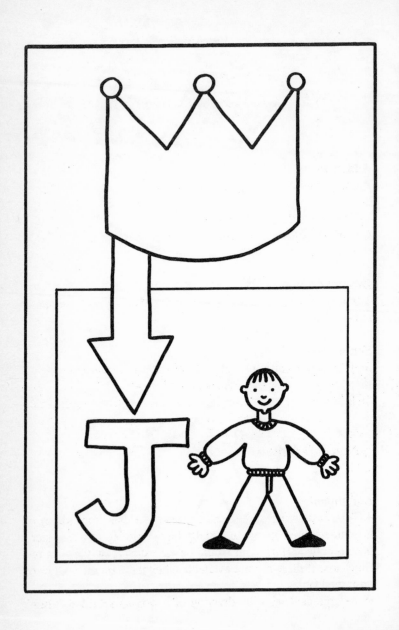

1 Corinthians 1:31 – What should we boast about?

Audience:
Primary school (older age-groups)

Learning Objective:
Christians believe that whoever wants to boast must boast of what the Lord has done.

Biblical basis:
1 Corinthians 1:31 – 'as it is written: "Let him who boasts boast in the Lord"'.[1]

Summary:
Step 1: Young children show off about what other people do.
Step 2: Older people show off about themselves.
Step 3: Christians believe that whoever wants to boast must boast of what the Lord has done.

Number of speakers:
One

Equipment:
● A large drawing of the head and arm of a four year-old boy on it (entitled 'Fred'); and an equally large drawing of a teenager's head (entitled 'Harry'). It would be easiest to draw these on two flipcharts. If these are not available, stick them on the wall or on up-turned tables.
● A large card with the drawing of a woman subtitled 'Mum',

and with a big tick alongside.

● A large card with a copy of Harry's face on it, with money visible in the background; the face should be sub-titled 'Me', and there should be a big tick alongside it.

● A large card with the word 'God' on it, and a big tick alongside it.

● A label with the word 'Christian' on it.

● Large cards (A3 size) on which short descriptions of what God has done are written. For example, 'God created the world'.

Script

Today we're going to be talking about 'showing off' *(introduce the concept of 'showing off' by giving an example of how you might show off, and then about how pupils might show off).*

Step 1: Young children show off about what other people do
I don't know if you've ever noticed, but really young children show off about different things to older people. Let me show you what I mean…

I'd like you to meet Fred *(turn page on the first flipchart to reveal 'Fred's' face and upper body).* Fred is four years old – he's several years younger than most of you here.

Fred is a bit of a show-off. However, he can't show off about himself, because he's not big, or strong *(point to thin arms)*, or very good at anything. So he doesn't show off about himself, but about other people. He says things like, 'My mummy is the bestest mummy there is.' If we were to draw what he's thinking when he's showing off, it would look like this...

(hold up large card with drawing of a woman sub-titled 'Mum', and a big tick alongside. Explain that this shows that he's showing off about his mother. Put the card on the flipchart – there's usually a sill on the frame that can be used for this. Option: you could draw think bubbles from Fred's head to the card to indicate that it's what he is thinking).

Step 2: Older people show off about themselves
Now let me introduce you to Harry *(reveal 'Harry's' face on the second flipchart).*

Harry is quite a bit older, and he's also a show-off. He shows off about himself, rather than about other people. He says things like '*I*'m really really good at computer games' and '*I*'ve got a harder punch than anyone else'. He also shows off about how much money he has. If we were to draw what he thinks like we did for Fred, it would look like this *(hold up the large card which has a big tick alongside the word 'Me', and then put it on the second flipchart).*

Step 3: Christians believe whoever wants to boast must boast of what the Lord has done.

The Bible talks about showing off, and it says that if we're going to show off, we should be showing off about someone else – God, in fact, and not showing off about ourselves.

Remember that four year-old Fred says things like 'My mummy is the bestest mummy'. Christians believe that, a bit like Fred, they should say things like, 'God is best; he's wonderful'. *(Hold up card with the word 'God' and a large tick alongside it. Put this over the card already on Fred's flipchart. Similarly replace Fred's name with the word 'Christian').*

Christians believe that there is a lot to show off about God. Let's think about a few of them…

(Ask for volunteers to come up and hold cards with phrases about how God is worthy of praise. For example, 'God created

the world',[2] 'God is love',[3] 'God's Son gave himself to rescue us'[4])

Christians believe God made the world in which we live. They believe that he loves us and wants us to know him. In fact, he loves us so much that he gave his Son Jesus to rescue us from doing wrong things that God hates. The Bible[5] says this: 'God loved the world so much that he gave his only Son, so that everyone who believes in him may not die but have eternal life'. What a wonderful God he is to do all these things for us!

Christians believe that what God has done for us is much more than we could ever do on our own. The Bible[6] says that: If anyone wants to 'show off',[7] they should show off about …God. So Christians believe that before God we should not be like Harry, who shows off about himself; instead, the Bible tells us to be like little children, who show off about what God has done. *(Point to the first flipchart which has a tick by the word 'God').*

Prayer:
Heavenly Father,
Please help us to know and remember how much you have done for us, and how much you have loved us.
Amen.

Song suggestion:
God is so good (composer unknown) *Junior Praise* No 53.

Options:

To increase time:

● Talk more about what God has done, perhaps using more cards.

● A song that could be sung as a solo (it probably won't be known by the pupils) is *There is no glory* by Debbye Graafsma:

There is no glory in my own wisdom,
there is no power in my own strength,
there is no might in my own riches,
but I will boast in knowing you.
For you are high and lifted up,
the glory of the nations,
you are high and lifted up,
the Lord of all the earth,
you are high and lifted up:
Creator, Redeemer, and I will boast in knowing you.

To shorten time:

● Do not ask for volunteers to come up to the front.

Fred

Harry

Mum

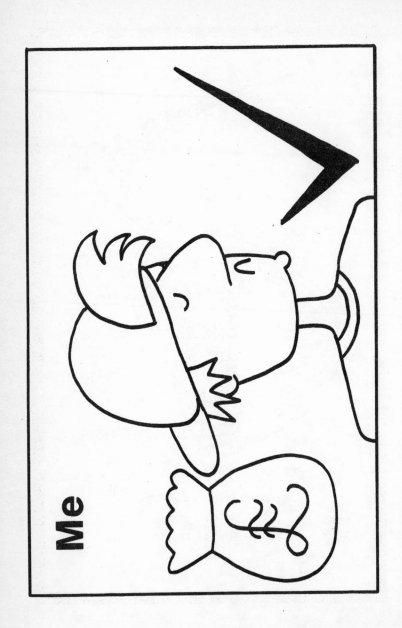

Romans 4:21 – Faith

Audience:
Primary school pupils

Learning objective:
Christians believe that faith is believing God's promises.

Biblical basis:
Romans 4:18-21 'Abraham believed and hoped, even when there was no reason for hoping... His faith did not leave him, and he did not doubt God's promise; his faith filled him with power, and he gave praise to God. He was absolutely sure that God would be able to do what he had promised.'[1]

Summary:
Introduction
Step 1: We are ready to believe things said by people we trust.
Step 2: Abraham was ready to believe things promised by God.
Step 3: Believing in God's promises is called 'faith'

Number of speakers:
One (but up to three could be usefully employed)

Equipment:
- 1 blindfold
- 3 pieces of brightly coloured cardboard (alternative: cushions)
- A roll of black bin liners (alternative: a large rug)

- Optional: White headdress and sheet
- Optional: Three signs – one saying 'Ur' with a picture of a town, one with a picture of the 'Promised Land', and one with a picture of a baby.

Comments:
Several volunteers are involved, and it would be helpful to have an adult assistant (perhaps a teacher?) to help marshal them.

Script

Before assembly starts lay out the bin liners in the centre of the presentation area with two 'stepping stones' of cardboard in the middle. There should be three chairs behind the area created by the bin liners.

Introduction
During assembly, whatever happens, we mustn't step onto the black area that I've laid out over the floor. Imagine that all sorts of nasty things are hiding in it, and so I mustn't step onto it… *(demonstrate teetering on the side).*

It's all right to step across the stepping stones – they are 'safe' – but not onto the black.

We're going to be using the stepping stones to help tell a story about what 'faith' is.
(Ask for two older volunteers from Year 6 and three younger volunteers. They should sit on some chairs to one side until required).

Step 1: We are ready to believe things said by people we trust.
(Ask the first of the Year 6 volunteers to step across the stepping stones, taking care not to fall into the black area. Once this is done, explain that you're going to make it more difficult. Blindfold the volunteer, then ask him or her to go over the steps again, giving clear instructions – 'now that you can't see, you'll have to trust me. Follow my voice; don't put your foot down firmly until I tell you that it's safe to do so'. When the task is successfully completed, ask the volunteer to sit back down in his or her original place.)

Step 2: Abraham was ready to believe things promised by God.
'I'm going to ask my second volunteer from Year 6 to do the same sort of thing, but he's going to do it as part of a story. It's a story from the Bible, and it's about a man called Abraham. Abraham lived in a hot country, so he had clothes to keep the sun off him *(put headdress on 'Abraham', and perhaps drape a sheet about him. Meanwhile, ask the younger volunteers to sit on the chairs beyond the black area, facing the rest of the pupils. Each one should hold one of the signs, initially turned to the blank side).*

Abraham lived in a town called Ur. Let's imagine that Ur is just here, right at the edge of the danger area. *(Ask 'volunteer 1' to turn his or her sign around: it says 'Ur').*

One day God said to Abraham: 'Leave your country and your house and go to the land I will show you.'[2] Abraham didn't know anything about this land he was supposed to go to, and he was going to have to trust God – like our other volunteer had to trust me earlier. So let's put a blindfold on 'Abraham'.

Now 'Abraham' can't see, and he has to trust that he's not going to step onto the black danger area, but is going to get to the land God promised *(Ask 'volunteer 2' to turn his or her sign around: it has a drawing with palm trees growing out of land. 'Abraham' is encouraged to take a step onto the first stepping stone).*

Some time after Abraham arrived at the Promised Land, God asked Abraham to make a further step. God promised that Abraham would have a son *(Ask 'volunteer 3' to turn his or her sign around: it shows a baby boy).*

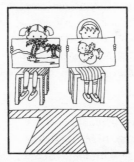

Now this seemed to be rather difficult, since Abraham was very old, and normally very old people can't have children. What's more, Abraham's wife thought that she could never become a mum. So it didn't seem possible that God could keep his promise that Abraham would have a son. But Abraham still trusted God.

(To 'Abraham') Abraham do you trust me? Can you make another step? Step carefully, and I'll tell you if you're going to go into the black area... *('Abraham' steps onto the next stepping stone).*

Brilliant! You made a 'step of faith', a bit like the real Abraham. He believed God's promise, and he did have a son. Thank you very much to my volunteers – please sit back down.

Step 3: Believing in God's promises is called 'faith'
Faith is believing God's promises – like Abraham believed God's promises. The Bible says that Abraham believed and hoped, even when there was no reason for hoping... His faith did not leave him, and he did not doubt God's promise. He was absolutely sure that God would be able to do what he had promised.[3]

Like Abraham, Christians today have faith in God. They believe in his promises – which are found in the Bible.

Optional prayer:
Heavenly Father,
Thank you that you make promises.
Please help us to believe in your promises, like Abraham did.
Amen.

Song suggestion:
Be bold, be strong (Morris Chapman) *Junior Praise* No 14

Options:
To reduce time:
● Cut out the dressing up of Abraham
● Cut out the younger volunteers and the signs
● Use an adult to do all the stepping across the 'stepping stones'.

To increase time:

● At the end of Step Three, give examples of the promises that are recorded in the Bible – for example, eternal life (John 3:16).

Comment:

Staging is an important consideration for this assembly. It will be difficult for pupils to see the stepping stones if the presentation area is small and on a level with the floor. If this is the case, consider using slightly raised cushions (keeping safety top of mind), or else have an adult assistant who is the one to be blindfolded and who acts up the difficulty of balancing. It would certainly be worth asking teachers' advice on how the assembly could best be staged.

John 21:1-6 – Trusting Jesus

Audience:
Infant school pupils

Learning objective:
Christians believe that we should listen to Jesus and follow what he says.

Biblical basis:
John 21: 6 'He *(Jesus)* said, "Throw your net on the right side of the boat, and you will find some." When they did, they were unable to haul the net in because of the large number of fish.'

Summary:
Step 1: Once there was a fisherman called Peter.
Step 2: In the Bible there is a story about Peter and Jesus.
Step 3: The story teaches us to listen to Jesus and follow what he says.

Number of speakers:
Two. In addition, the (non-speaking) help of another adult is recommended; perhaps a teacher might be enlisted.

Equipment required:
- Two or three fishing nets (alternative: large hairnets)
- Several cardboard cut-outs of fish, ideally of different colours
- Three chairs; on the back of one there should be a large sheet

of paper with a cross drawn on it
- *Optional:* Fishing rod made out of rolled newspaper and string
- Fisherman-type clothes for 'Peter'
- Large cardboard box for 'Peter's' boat

Comments:
- An ideal time for this assembly would be shortly after Easter.
- The (non-speaking) adult to play 'Jesus'.

Script

In the centre of presentation area place cardboard box to represent fishing boat. At the back of the box, invisible to pupils, put a net full of cardboard cutouts of fish. At one side there should be two chairs ready for 'Peter's' friends; on the other side a single chair for 'Jesus'.

Step 1: The Bible has a story of people who went fishing
In today's assembly, we're going to be thinking about someone who was a fisherman. Some of you might have gone fishing for fun, but fishing was this person's job. His name was Peter. My friend *(point to co-presenter)* is going to be Peter for today. He was a big man and he had large muscles *('Peter' flexes muscles)* because he used to lift up nets full of fish.

oilskins (like a fisherman)

Step 2: In the Bible there is a story about Peter and Jesus.
Peter was a friend of Jesus – in fact, he was one of Jesus' best friends. We're going to tell a story about Peter *(point to 'Peter')* and Jesus *(point to 'Jesus')* in this assembly. *(Explain that you'll also need two volunteers to help with the story – they represent 'friends of Peter'. They should be sitting on chairs at the front until needed).*

One day Peter met Jesus. Peter knew Jesus was a very special person, so he decided to leave his job as a fisherman and instead went about with Jesus *('Peter' shakes hands with 'Jesus' and they walk about).* But you may have already have heard Bible stories about what happened to Jesus – he was killed. *(to 'Jesus')* Could you sit down for a time, to represent the fact that Jesus was killed – but don't worry – you still have a part, because Jesus comes back to life. *('Jesus' sits on the chair with the cross on it).*

Peter was scared when Jesus was killed; he thought he might be killed too. So he went back to his old job. He went back to being a fisherman. *('Peter' goes over to his 'boat').*

One day shortly afterwards something rather odd happened whilst Peter was fishing. He was out in his boat with some friends *(the two volunteers stand beside 'Peter' in his 'boat').*

The way they used to fish at the time when this story happened was with nets. Peter, can you show your friends how to fish with a net?

('Peter' mimes scooping up fish with the net. He gives nets to his 'friends', as well as other props – for example a fishing rod made out of rolled newspaper and string. He should ensure they all fish over the left side of the boat).

On this particular day, Peter and his friends are fishing, but they don't catch anything. *('Peter' mimes trying to scoop up fish, and looks disappointedly at his friends).*

They put their net into the water again and again, but no fish were caught. Night came, and still they fished. They fished all night *('Peter' yawns)*. But still no fish.

At last the night was over and the sun came up. Then a very special person appeared at the water's edge. It was somebody who had been killed, but had then come back to life. *(Lead 'Jesus' closer to the 'boat').*

Let me tell you what happened next:

MAIN PRESENTER: *(reading from Bible)* 'As the sun was rising, Jesus stood at the water's edge, but the disciples in the boat did not know that it was Jesus. Then Jesus asked them, 'Young men, haven't you caught anything?' *('Jesus' could mime shouting over water by cupping his hands around his mouth).*

'PETER': Not a thing – and we've been fishing all night.

MAIN PRESENTER: Jesus said to them: 'Throw your net out on the right side of the boat, and you'll catch some fish.'

'PETER': *(to his friends)* Well, this is a strange thing, isn't it. We've been out here all night and haven't caught a thing, and now that man over there – I don't know who he is – says we should throw the net over to the other side. Well, I suppose we could try it...

('Peter' scoops his net on the other side of the 'boat'. He exchanges the empty net for one full of cardboard fish which is hidden behind the 'boat').

'PETER': I don't believe it! We've got lots and lots of fish. I don't know if I can pull the net back in, it's so full and heavy *(mimes difficulty in raising the net).*

Do you know what... I think I recognise that man. It's Jesus! It's the Lord! Hang on Lord, I'm coming over to you...

MAIN PRESENTER: Freeze! *(points at 'Peter', who freezes).* Now what's going on?

Step 3: The story teaches us to listen to Jesus and follow what he says.

Christians believe that the story shows us that it's a good idea to listen to Jesus and follow what he says. Imagine that when Jesus first called out to Peter, Peter hadn't listened. Things would have been very different then. Let's rewind the story so far as if the action was on a video, and see what would have happened. We'll go back to when Peter was sitting in the boat waiting to catch some fish:

('Peter' swims backwards to the boat and takes the cardboard fish out of the net.)

Let's go back to the stage where Jesus appears at the water's edge.

(Picks up Bible)

MAIN PRESENTER: Jesus stood at the water's edge, but the disciples in the boat did not know that it was Jesus. Then Jesus asked them, 'Young men, haven't you caught anything?'

PETER: Not a thing – and we've been fishing all night.

MAIN PRESENTER: Jesus said to them: 'Throw your net out on the right side of the boat, and you'll catch some fish.'

'PETER': *(to his friends)* Well, this is a strange thing, isn't it. We've been out here all night and haven't caught a thing, and now that man over there – I don't know who he is – says we should throw the net over to the other side. I don't think we should do that, do you? No, let's not listen to him. *(makes dismissive gesture towards 'Jesus').*

MAIN PRESENTER: Well, that wouldn't have been very good at all, would it? Peter would not have caught any fish if he had ignored Jesus and continued to fish in his own way.

But that wasn't what happened. Peter did listen to Jesus, he did throw his net out on the other side even though he couldn't see that it would make any difference.

Christians believe that the story of Peter's fish is a picture of how all of us should listen to Jesus, and follow what he says. Jesus promises us that if we do listen and follow him, as Peter did, then we'll be given much more than fish; we'll be friends with God forever. That's a very wonderful thing.
(Thank volunteers for their help and ask them to sit down).

Optional prayer
God our Heavenly Father,
Thank you that you are interested in each one of us.
Please help us to listen to Jesus, and to follow what he says.
Amen.

Song suggestion:
God is so good (composer unknown) *Junior Praise* No 53

Options:
To reduce time:
● Don't ask for volunteers to act as 'friends of Peter'.
● The presenter could paraphrase the 'rewind' section.

To increase time:
● Personal experience of how you listen to Jesus as a Christian today (through the Bible, prayer); this could be talked about after the volunteers have sat back down.

Other options:
● Staging could be more elaborate – for example, benches could be put either side of the 'boat', and cardboard cut-outs in the shape of waves could be laid against them.

John 3:16 – Easter assembly

Audience:
Middle school pupils

Learning objective:
Christians believe that God loved the world so much that he gave his only Son.

Biblical basis:
John 3:16 'For God so loved the world that he gave his one and only Son...'

Summary:
Introduction
Step 1: God created the world and it was good
Step 2: However, mankind rebelled against God
Step 3: God punishes this rebellion...
Step 4: ...yet out of love he sent his Son Jesus to change this situation
Step 5: Jesus died for us, then rose again
Step 6: People now have a choice to make

Number of speakers:
One – but a second adult would help to represent 'God' as the part requires standing about without fidgeting.

Equipment:
● Two polystyrene cups connected by a piece of string

approximately four-and-a-half feet long.
- Sign saying 'Heaven'
- Sign saying 'Earth' and with a smiling face on it on one side, and on the other side, the word 'Earth' and a serious face.
- Large scissors
- A cross
- One or more benches. These should be available from the school, but if not, an alternative would be to use a large cushion.

Comments:
This assembly was mentioned in chapter 2.

Script

Introduction
(Ask for three volunteers amongst older pupils. Then hold up two polystyrene cups connected by a piece of string and explain that this is a simple telephone. Demonstrates how the 'telephone' works with one of the volunteers).

We're going to use this simple telephone to tell a Bible story. I'd like you to use your imaginations for this story.

Tell the volunteers where to stand. Before assembly you should place three benches at the front; they should be joined lengthways and have a sign saying 'Heaven'. The volunteer representing 'God' stands on the bench; 'Jesus' sits cross-legged on the bench. The volunteer representing 'people' sits directly below 'God' about two feet forward of the bench, close to a large sign saying 'Earth' and with a smiling face drawn on it.

Step 1: God created the world and it was good

Christians believe that 'In the beginning, God...' *(point to 'God')* '...created the heavens' *(point to the benches and the sign)* 'and the earth'[1] *(point towards the sign on the floor)*. He created people[2] who live on the earth – and I'd like you to imagine that the volunteer sitting on the floor represents 'people'.

To begin with, Christians believe that God and people were good friends. To show this, I'll give one end of our simple telephone to 'God', and the other to the people. You can see that whenever God talks, people can easily hear – could you give a demonstration of that please?

...And also, it's easy for people to talk with God.

Step 2: However, mankind rebelled against God

That was how it was to begin with. But the Bible tells us that one day people turned away from God, and didn't want to listen any more to what he said.[3] To show this, I'm going to give a pair of scissors to 'people'. Why don't you cut the string – then you can be sure that you won't have to be bothered by God any more.

Step 3: God punishes this rebellion...
'People no longer listened to God. Christians believe that they became enemies of God, and they also believe that God punishes his enemies.[4] Things were spoilt[5] *(turn the sign 'Earth' around to show an unsmiling face)*, and all sorts of bad things went on amongst them.[6]
(Ask 'God' to talk into his cup, and as he does this hold up the loose end to show that the link between God and men is now cut).

Step 4: ...yet out of love he sent his Son Jesus to change this situation
This was a big problem. But Christians believe that God had a plan to save people from being punished. The Bible says that God loved the world so much that he gave his only Son, so that everyone who believes in him may not die but have eternal life.[7]

(Ask 'Jesus' to go down to 'earth' and tie the two loose ends of string back together. Explain that this is a bit like Jesus, God's Son).

Step 5: Jesus died for us, then rose again

Tying the loose ends togther was a fairly easy thing for our volunteer to do, but it wasn't as easy for Jesus to repair the link between God and man. Christians believe that nothing less than Jesus' death could change the way things were. It will soon be Easter, and one of the special days of Easter is Good Friday. Good Friday is when Christians remember that Jesus died on the cross. *(Hold up a simple cross)*. And Christians believe that he did this so that people could be friends with God again.[8] *(Hold the knot in your other hand)*.

On the third day after Jesus died, Christians believe that he came back to life and went up to heaven *('Jesus' is asked to stand on the right of 'God' on the bench)*. We remember him coming back to life on Easter Sunday – the third day after Good Friday.

Step 6: People now have a choice to make
What happened at the first Easter has made a big difference. Christians believe that now people have a choice of two things they can do. Either they can continue to ignore God and do their own thing, just like people did in the past. Christians believe that if they do that, they'll still be enemies of God, and that's a bad thing to be. Or, they can turn back to God… *(take up the cup and put it to your ear)* …and be friends with God – because of what Jesus has done.

Optional prayer:
Heavenly Father,
Thank you for making us.
Thank you that we can be friends with you because of Jesus.
Please help us to know you more.
Amen.

Song suggestion:
Jesus is a friend of mine (Paul Mazak) *Junior Praise* No 136

Options:

To reduce time

● If there is insufficient time, it might be worth saving this assembly for another time when it could be done in its entirety – go prepared with a shorter 'Plan B'.

To increase time

● Include a short personal statement of faith during the last step.

Earth

:)

Earth

Part Three

Useful contacts

This lists some of the national and local organisations involved in schools work. For detailed information about what is going on in your area, it is worth asking the Schools Ministry Network (SMN). This is an umbrella organisation for schools work, and it should be able to identify your local contacts.

The addresses are divided into groups:
1. Schools Ministry Network
2. National organisations involved in schools work
3. Relevant national organisations
4. Local organisations and groups
5. Training Centres
6. Government organisations

1.   Schools Ministry Network

Schools Ministry Network
The Administrator
207 Queensway
Bletchley
Milton Keynes MK2 2EB
Tel: 01908 856000
Fax: 01908 856111

The Schools Ministry Network (SMN) is a voluntary association of Christian organisations and individuals working with schools. In joining the network, members commit themselves to its objectives, principles, and practice.

Objectives of SMN:

1. To promote integrity of Christian ministry in schools, and appropriate standards of practice.
2. To co-operate for strategic planning and placement of people and resources.
3. To share resources and ideas, provide credibility, and give opportunities for fellowship and training.
4. To encourage a wider involvement of Christian churches and organisations in ministry in schools.

Principles and practice

Members of the network:

(1) recognise schools to be places of education and seek to work with them in appropriate ways;

(2) believe Christians have a responsibility to make a positive contribution to the whole school community;

(3) seek to assist pupils to evaluate Christianity as a way of life by, for example:

(a) helping them understand the basic Christian beliefs;

(b) sharing the relevance of Christianity to different areas of life;

(c) assisting pupils in forming and/or clarifying personal values;

(d) supporting on-going Christian work in schools;

(e) giving pupils a positive experience of meeting Christians;

(f) bringing personal and professional support for Christian teachers;

Network members also:

(4) recognise the importance of a strategic, long-term approach and ministry in the school community;

(5) seek to work in conjunction with, and mindful of, the school staff and not in isolation;

(6) seek to co-operate with other Christians in the school community;

(7) seek to identify and make contact with Christians already working in a school before beginning something new;

(8) show respect for school administration, staff and parents, and never knowingly undermine them;

(9) seek to teach Christian principles, while not promoting denominations;

(10) aim to be united in purpose yet affirm our diversity in approach and style, within the parameters of the above.

Basis of Membership

A belief in God – the Father,
His Son Jesus Christ, as Lord and Saviour,
the Holy Spirit

A conviction that the Bible forms the
basis of our beliefs and lifestyle

Membership does not imply that any individual has undergone any particular training or is accredited in any way. Members are ultimately responsible to their own employers or organisations.

2. National Organisations involved in schools work

Scripture Union (with a network of schools workers. Also support materials for Christian groups in schools)
207 - 209 Queensway
Bletchley
Milton Keynes
Buckinghamshire MK2 2EB
Tel: 01908 856000
Fax: 01908 856111

Youth for Christ (with a network of schools workers, as well as a music group ('TVB') and 'Activate' theatre company)
PO Box 5254
Halesowen
West Midlands B63 3DG
Tel: 0121 550 8055
Fax: 0121 550 9979

Crusaders (has a number of schools workers)
2 Romeland Hill
St Albans
Hertfordshire AL3 4BR
Tel: 01727 855422
Fax: 01727 848518

Discovery (has teams of schools workers based in Birmingham and South London: looking to expand to other cities)
Fairgate House
Kings Road
Tyseley
Birmingham B11 2AA
Tel: 0121 4413364

Oasis Trust (provides personnel and resources to churches in their involvement with local schools. A schools mission team is also available)
87 Blackfriars Road
London SE1 8HA
Tel: 0171 928 9422

Youth With A Mission (YWAM)
Highfield Oval
Ambrose Lane
Harpenden
Hertfordshire AL5 4BX
Tel: 01582 765481
Fax: 01582 768048

Open Air Campaigners (has a number of schools workers)
102 Dukes Avenue
Muswell Hill
London N10 2QA
Tel: 0181 444 5254

The Gideons International in the British Isles (distributes Bibles
in schools)
Western House
George Street
Lutterworth
Leicestershire LE17 4EE
Tel: 01455 554241

3. Relevant national organisations

Association of Christian Teachers (fellowship, advice and
support for Christian teachers, as well as short courses on
educational topics)
94A London Road
St Albans
Hertfordshire AL1 1NX
Tel: 01727 840298
Fax: 01727 848966

CARE for Education (aims to serve Christians involved in
eduction – parents, teachers, governors, church leaders – through
providing training and resources)
53 Romney Street
London SW1P 3RF
Tel: 0171 233 0455
Fax: 0171 233 0983

The National Society (Church of England body concerned with supporting church schools, RE and parish education)
Church House
Great Smith Street
London SW1P 3NZ
Tel: 0171 222 1672
Fax: 0171 233 2592

4. Local organisations and groups

This a selection of some of the organisations that I have contacted, listed by area. It does not consititute an exhaustive list. Some of the groups may be willing to travel to other nearby districts.

Cambridgeshire

Christian Options in Peterborough Schools (CROPS)
Adderley
North Bretton
Peterborough PE3 8RA
Tel: 01733 266915

Cumbria/N Lancashire/W Yorkshire

North West Evangelistic Trust (network of eight schools workers)
Warehouse Christian Centre
Preston Street
Carnforth
Lancashire LA5 9DB
Tel: 01524 732764

Derbyshire

Christians Involved in Derbyshire Schools (CIDS)
c/o Mr G. Hunt
9 Paxton Close
Matlock
Derbyshire DE4 3TD
Tel: 01629 56906

Kent

The Family Trust
St Luke's Church
St Luke's Road
Maidstone
Kent ME14 5AR
Tel: 01622 687074

London

Brent Association for Christian Education
c/o Mr Henderson Springer
Tel: 0181 902 0755

Spinaker Trust
Coppice Hall
Hollingworth Road
Petts Wood
Orpington
Kent BR5 1AQ
0181 295 1654

South London Schools Project
c/o Youth for Christ
St Michaels' House
2 Elizabeth Street
London SW1W 9RB
Tel: 0171 730 4113

Nottinghamshire
Christian Education in Nottingham Schools (CENS Trust)
c/o Mr Chris Chesterton
232 Westdale Lane
Carlton
Nottingham NG4 4FW
Tel: 01159 606228
Internet: www.innotts.co.uk/~cens

Suffolk

Ipswich Christian Youth Ministries (CYM)
6 Great Colman Street
Ipswich IP4 2AD
Tel: 01473 216712

Tyne and Wear

Christians and Tyneside Schools (CATS)
Eslington House
Eslington Terrace
Jesmond
Newcastle-upon-Tyne NE2 4RF
Tel: 0191 281 5664
Fax: 0191 281 4272

Northern Ireland

Logos Ministries
147 Albertbridge Road
Belfast BT5 4PS
Tel: 01232 458362

5. Other contacts for training

A number of the organisations already listed are involved in training: the best thing to do is to ask for advice from the Schools Ministry Network on your most local contacts.

In addition:

St John's Extension Studies (runs 'Worship that Works' correspondence course)
Bramcote
Nottingham NG9 3DS
Tel: 0115 251117

Janet King (a freelance trainer and consultant on Religious Education and 'collective worship', and has written a number of assembly books)
Violet Cottage
41 Upland Road
Thornwood Common
Nr Epping
Essex CM16 6NJ
Tel: 01992 578164

6. Government organisations

Department for Education and Employment
Public Enquiry Unit
Sanctuary Building
Great Smith Street
London SW1T 3DT
Tel: 0171 925 5555
Fax: 0171 925 6971/6960

Useful Resources

1. Resource Groups

Viz-a-Viz (national team available for school missions, using creative media and contemporary presentations)
227 Rayleigh Road
Hutton
Brentwood
Essex CM3 1PJ
Tel: 01277 215222

Hands and Feet (Creative Communication)
5 Arnesby Road
Nottingham NG7 2EA
Tel: 0115 9782249

Riding Lights Theatre Company
8 Bootham Terrace
York YO3 7DH
Tel: 01904 655317
Fax: 01904 651532

Children Worldwide (produce resources for assemblies)
Dalesdown
Honeybridge Lane
Dial Post
Horsham
West Sussex RH13 8NX
Tel: 014037 101712

Footprints Theatre Co
St Nicholas Centre
79 Maid Marian Way
Nottingham NG1 6AE
Tel: 0115 9586554

Saltmine Trust (drama, music: willing to travel)
PO Box 15
Dudley
West Midlands DY3 2AN
Tel: 01902 881080
Fax: 01902 881099

One Way UK (puppets and resources)
41 Hollydale Close
Reading
Berkshire RG2 8LL
Tel: 01734 756303

2. Resource Centres

Stapleford House Resource Centre (resources and training to
support Religious Education and 'collective worship')
Wesley Place
Stapleford
Nottingham NG9 8PD
Tel: 0115 9396270

Note:
1. The Stapleford Project is organising a scheme whereby churches can support local schools with resources – please contact them for more information.
2. A termly magazine for primary schools is now being produced – *Cracking RE*. It is aimed at classroom teachers. Each issue contains twelve assemblies with photocopiable illustrations.

National Society RE Centre
36 Causton Street
London SW1P 4AU
Tel: 0171 932 1190

Diocesan Resource Centres (Anglican)
Many Anglican dioceses have RE Resource Centres. Details are available from local telephone directories.

Diocesan Religious Education Centres (Roman Catholic)
Details are available from diocesan directories or telephone directories.

Schools Christian Resource Centre (supporting schools in Merton & Sutton)
68 Middleton Road
Morden
Surrey SM4 6RS
Tel: 0181 640 8853

Christian Resources Project
14 Lipson Road
Plymouth
Devon PL4 8PW
Tel: 01752 224012

3. Books

There is a variety of books available to support 'collective worship'. Most Christian bookshops have a fair selection – which ones you prefer depends very much on personal style and taste. Scripture Union produces a number of resources, listed in its *Children's Catalogue*. The Stapleford Project (Association of Christian Teachers) also has a range of materials – see above.

The Schools Work Handbook by Emlyn Williams and published by Scripture Union is a useful guide covering a wide range of ways in which Christians can assist schools.

If you would like details of further resources brought out by the author of this book please contact him c/o Monarch Publications.

Part Four
Appendices

APPENDIX 1

Useful facts about schools

It doesn't seem that long since I left school, but the way that year groups are numbered, the names of exams, and almost everything else seems to have changed. If you're a parent you may be fully aware of the new jargon; this appendix as it is really for the benefit of those who have had less contact with schools and consequently talk about the '5th form' rather than Year 11, and who muddle up their Key Stages.

1. Year Numberings

Year Numbering	Age of pupils	Former Year Numbering
Reception	5 or under	
Year 1	5 – 6	Varied
Year 2	6 – 7	Varied
Year 3	7 – 8	Varied
Year 4	8 – 9	Varied
Year 5	9 – 10	Varied
Year 6	10 – 11	Varied
Year 7	11 – 12	1st form
Year 8	12 – 13	2nd form
Year 9	13 – 14	3rd form
Year 10	14 – 15	4th form
Year 11	15 – 16	5th form
Year 12 (Lower 6th)	16 – 17	Lower 6th
Year 13 (Upper 6th)	17 – 18	Upper 6th

2. Key Stages

The National Curriculum brought in 'key stages' for learning.

Years	Key Stage
Reception	*n/a*
Years 1 & 2	Key Stage 1
Years 3, 4, 5, 6	Key Stage 2
Years 7, 8, 9	Key Stage 3
Years 10, 11	Key Stage 4
Years 12, 13	*n/a*

3. Exams

Name of exam	Age of pupils	What has been replaced
GCSE	16	O-Level and CSE
A-Level	18	
AS-Level	18	new (equivalent to half an A-Level)

4. Types of schools

Organisation of schools by age-groups varies across the country. In some places there is a straightforward 'primary' and 'secondary' split, but elsewhere the picture is more complex. Some of the more common variations are shown opposite.

Year Numbering	Age of pupils			
Reception	5 or under	Primary	Infants	First school
Year 1	5 – 6			
Year 2	6 – 7			
Year 3	7 – 8		Junior	
Year 4	8 – 9			
Year 5	9 – 10			Middle school
Year 6	10 – 11			
Year 7	11 – 12	Secondary	Senior	
Year 8	12 – 13			
Year 9	13 – 14			High school
Year 10	14 – 15			
Year 11	15 – 16			
Year 12 (Lower 6th)	16 – 17		6th form college	
Year 13 (Upper 6th)	17 – 18			

APPENDIX II

What about other faiths?

This summarises how current legislation and guidelines envisage 'collective worship' will work in the context of large numbers of pupils either from other faiths or of no faith.

Circular 1/94 argues that the legal requirement for collective worship which is 'wholly or mainly of a broadly Christian character' should be appropriate for most pupils across the country. Nevertheless, it is not forced on pupils whose parents have objections. Parents have a right to withdraw their children from collective worship if they wish. In addition, head teachers can apply for an exemption from broadly Christian collective worship (a 'determination'), either for the whole school or for a clearly described and defined group.

Exercise of right of withdrawal

Circular 1/94 states that 'the parental right to withdraw a child from attending collective worship should be freely exercisable and a school must give effect to any such request.'

Paragraph 87 says 'Experience suggests that, to avoid misunderstanding, a head teacher will find it helpful to establish with any parent wanting to exercise the right of withdrawal:
- the elements of worship in which the parent would object to the child taking part;
- the practical implications of withdrawal; and
- whether the parent will require any advanced notice of such worship, and, if so, how much.'

'Determinations' (exemptions from broadly Christian collective worship)

Circular 1/94 recognises that there could be conflict between two of its guidelines. Paragraph 60 states 'in the light of the Christian traditions of Great Britain, section 7(1) of the Education Reform Act ... says that collective worship organised by a county or equivalent grant-maintained school is to be "wholly or mainly of a broadly Christian character."'

Paragraph 64, meanwhile, states 'The extent to which and the ways in which the broad traditions of Christian belief are to be reflected in such acts of collective worship should be appropriate to the family backgrounds of the pupils and their ages and aptitudes. It is for the head teacher to determine this after consultation with the governing body.'

In schools where these two requirements conflict, an exemption or 'determination' can be applied for, either for the whole school, or for a clearly defined group within the school.

If a head teacher does decide to seek a determination, he or she can apply to the local Standing Advisory Council on Religious Education (SACRE) to lift or modify the normal requirements for collective worship. One factor which may inform a head teacher's decision to make an application to the SACRE is the extent of withdrawals from broadly Christian collective worship. The SACRE will grant the 'determination' according to circumstances relating to the family backgrounds of the pupils concerned.

On a personal note, in my research I have come across schools which have not applied for a determination despite a high proportion of pupils from a non-Christian faith. For example, the headmistress of a school where over 50% of the pupils are from an Asian background says: 'Asian parents often want their child to go to our church school as they seek religious and moral emphasis in their education.'

Her school is judged to fully comply with the requirement for broadly Christian collective worship.

This appendix should not treated as giving legal advice. Further information can be obtained from the Department for Education and Employment (Tel: 0171 925 5555).

Extract from 1988 Education Reform Act

This extract from the 1988 Education Reform Act is a key piece of legislation governing collective worship in county schools:

7. Special provisions as to collective worship in county schools

(1) Subject to the following provisions of this section, in the case of a county school the collective worship required in the school by section 6 of this Act shall be wholly or mainly of a broadly Christian character.

(2) For the purposes of subsection (1) above, collective worship is of a broadly Christian character if it reflects the broad traditions of Christian belief without being distinctive of any particular Christian denomination.

(3) Every act of collective worship required by section 6 of this Act in the case of a country school need not comply with subsection (1) above provided that, taking any school term as a whole, most such acts which take place in the school do comply with that subsection.

(4) Subject to subsections (1) and (3) above:

(a) the extent to which (if at all) any acts of collective worship required by section 6 of this Act which do not comply with subsection (1) above take place in a county school;

(b) the extent to which any act of collective worship in a county school

which complies with subsection (1) above reflects the broad traditions of Christian belief; and

(c) the ways in which those traditions are reflected in any such act of
collective worship;

shall be such as may be appropriate having regard to any relevant
considerations relating to the pupils concerned which fail to be taken
into account in accordance with subsection (5) below.

(5) Those considerations are:

(a) any circumstances relating to the family backgrounds of the pupils
concerned which are relevant for determining the character of the
collective worship which is appropriate in their case; and

(b) their ages and aptitudes

(6) Where under section 12 of this Act a standing advisory council on
religious education determine that it is not appropriate for subsection
(1) above to apply in the case of any county school, or in the case of
any class or description of pupils at such a school, then, so long as that
determination has effect:

(a) that subsection shall not apply in relation of that school or (as the
case may be) in relation to those pupils; and

(b) the collective worship required by section 6 of this Act in the case
of that school of those pupils shall not be distinctive of any
particular Christian or other regligious denomination (but this shall
not be taken as preventing that worship from being distinctive of
any particular faith).

Sub-s (1) The collective worship required in country schools 'shall be
wholly or mainly of a broadly Christian character' which means (see
sub-s (2)) that the collective worship 'reflects the broad traditions of
Christian belief without being distinctive of any particular Christian
denomination'.

Sub-s (3) It is not necessary for every act of collective worship to
comply with subsection (1) if, 'taking any school term as a whole, most
... such acts which take place in the school to comply with that
subsection'.

Sub-s (4) Introduces some latitude having regard to any of the 'relevant considerations' set out in subsection (5), namely (a) 'any circumstances relating to the family backgrounds of the pupils concerned which are relevant for determining the character of the collective worship which is appropriate in their case; and (b) 'their ages and aptitudes'.

For a case in which sub-s (1) to (4) were considered, see *R v Secretary of State for Education, ex p Ruscoe* (1993), **F(111)**.

Sub-s (6) Provides that, under section 12, a standing advisory council on religious education may exempt from the requirements of sub-s (1) any county school or any class or description of pupils at a county school.

APPENDIX IV

Applying to become a charity

Christian groups concerned with education can apply to become registered charities. This appendix briefly explains why and how this might be done. It does not constitute legal advice.

I am grateful to David Jones of UKET (United Kingdom Evangelization Trust) for providing much of the information.

When does the law require a Christian group concerned with education to become a charity?

Registration is necessary when any of the following become true of the group...

...your annual income is greater than £1000 a year

...you occupy a rateable property solely for the purpose of administering your group

...a permanent endowment has been left to the group due to someone's Will

Registration if any of the above conditions are met is not optional – the 1993 Charities Act requires it!

There may be an exception if your group falls entirely within one main line denomination. If this is the case, check the Charity Commissioners' leaflet *Registration of Religious Charities* (CC22). Their contact details are at the end of this appendix.

What are the benefits and disadvantages of registering as a charity?

Benefits

✓ **Increases funding** – charities can receive donations through Deed of Covenant and Gift Aid, which means that tax can be recovered.

✓ **Increases credibility** – charities are accountable to trustees, and this helps reassure donors that their money is going to a bonafide organisation. In addition, other Christian Trusts that you might want to ask for support may be more likely to give to another charity than to a non-charity.

✓ **Decreases risk of mismanagement** – a Trust Deed provides a sound and flexible legal framework for the financial affairs of your group. Trustees have a duty to ensure good management.

Disadvantages

✗ **Cost and complexity of applying for charitable status** – A Trust Deed needs to be submitted to the Charity Commissioners. Legal advice is not essential, but may be helpful in speeding agreement to the Deed. Legal costs will vary between £200 – £500.

✗ **Proof must be kept of prudent management** – Simplified accounts, including a receipts and payments account and a statement of assets and liabilities, must be kept. However, they only need to be examined by an 'independent examiner' if income exceeds £10,000 per annum. There should be at least an annual meeting of the trustees, with minutes kept.

✗ **Trustees may be liable if the charity makes a loss** – There are two areas of liability:
- Trustees may have to honour financial commitments made by the charity if its funds run out.
- Trustees may be liable to make up money that was spent on something outside the charity's purpose.
  For example, if the charity's money was spent on party political campaigns when the purpose of the charity was to 'advance the Christian faith in schools and churches in the local area', trustees might be liable for repaying the misspent money.

How do you go about setting up a charity?

A draft Trust Deed needs to be submitted to the Charity Commissioners together with replies to a detailed questionnaire about the activities and structures of your group. For further information and a sample Trust Deed please contact UKET.

Once approved by the Commissioners, a Trust Deed can be formally signed and completed and the charity registered. The procedure will usually take six months with legal advice, and longer without this.

What is the role of trustees?

Charity trustees are the persons having the general control and management of a charity. It's a responsible position! Most charities have between three (the legal minimum) and ten trustees (the maximum for easy management). They should 'exercise the same degree of care in dealing with the administration of their charity as a prudent man of business would exercise in carrying out his own or his business affairs'.

Useful information for trustees

1. Charities do not pay VAT on promotional material or new buildings.
2. Your bank should be asked to pay interest gross, rather than net of tax as usual, since charities are exempt from income tax.
3. Reclaiming tax on Covenants/Gift Aid can be done several times in each tax year – you do not have to wait until the year end.

Who should be chosen as a trustee?

Trustees need to be able to give the necessary time and attention to managing the charity, and to be committed to its vision. Professional expertise is not a requirement, but can be an asset.

Trustees should not obtain any benefit from their Trust, except for reasonable out of pocket expenses. It is therefore not appropriate for any worker who is paid by the Trust to also be a trustee.

If you have queries on this or any aspect of charity formation, the organisations listed overleaf should be able to assist you further:

Charity Commissioners:

London
St Albans House
57-60 Haymarket
London SW1Y 4QX
Tel: 0171 210 4477
Fax: 0171 930 9173

Liverpool
2nd Floor
20 Kings Parade
Queens Dock
Liverpool L3 4DQ
Tel: 0151 703 1500
Fax: 0151 703 1555

Taunton
Woodfield House
Tangier
Taunton
Somerset TA1 4BL
Tel: 01823 345000
Fax: 01823 345003

United Kingdom Evangelization Trust (UKET)

PO Box 99
Loughton
Essex IG10 3QJ
Tel: 0181 505 5600
Fax: 0181 502 5333
E-mail: 100416,710@compuserve.com

UKET offers legal services (including charity formation) to churches and Christian organisations. Additional services include the administration of Covenant and Gift Aid Accounts, insurance agency services, taxation service to Christian workers, Trust Fund administration, and mortgages and loans to churches and Christian organisations.

Notes

Chapter 1
1 'Guidance on the Inspection of Secondary Schools', HMSO 1995. p89
2 Inspection Report p16
3 Source: OFSTED. Figures quoted by David Trainor at a meeting of the Parliamentary Christian Fellowship 19/6/95
4 Figures rounded to nearest hundred
5 Source: OFSTED. Figures quoted by David Trainor at a meeting of the Parliamentary Christian Fellowship 19/6/95
6 Figures rounded to nearest hundred
7 Genesis 1:1 (NIV)
8 Genesis 1:26-27
9 Genesis 3
10 Romans 1:18-32
11 Genesis 1:17-19
12 Luke 19:27
13 John 3:16
14 1 Peter 3:18
15 Gallup Poll 1993. Quoted in *The Times*, 29/6/95

Chapter 2
1 See the transcript of a meeting of the Parliamentary Christian Fellowship 19/6/95, chaired by the Bishop of Ripon

2 *Ibid* p 2

3 *Ibid* p 4

4 Ryle Commentary on Matthew 7:6, p 63

5 cf St Paul: 'I gave you milk, not solid food, for you were not yet ready for it.' 1 Corinthians 3:2

6 Acts 17

7 Rev M. Leonard in *Scouts Own*. First published 1933

8 James 3:4-5 (NIV) – my italics

9 Published by Navpress

Chapter 4

1 John Burn

Chapter 5

1 The addresses of the church leaders (mainly evangelicals) came from the Christian Research Association

2 Teachers within the congregation were specifically excluded, as they are not 'visitors' to schools

Jesus' humility

1 Based on John 13:12-17, Good News

Active response

1 Luke 10:25-37

2 Luke 10:37

The rich man and Lazarus

1 More practical examples of this could be added

2 The original listeners included the Pharisees who 'sneered at Jesus, because they loved money' (Luke 16:14)

3 Luke 16:19-31

4 The word is 'Hades' in the Good News, 'hell' in the NIV

God as creator

1 NIV

2 Good News

3 Genesis 1:1-3 NIV

4 Genesis 1:3
5 St Paul
6 Quoted from *The Message*, Navpress (based on Romans 1:20)
7 cf Acts 17:24

Rest from life's burdens
1 NIV
2 Matthew 11:28 Good News

How can we know God
1 NIV

What should we boast about?
1 NIV
2 Genesis 1:1
3 1 John 4:16
4 Based on Galatians 1:4 – '…the Lord Jesus Christ, who gave himself for our sins to rescue us from the present evil age…'
5 John 3:16 Good News
6 Based on Jeremiah 9:24. See also 1 Corinthians 1:31 – 'Whoever wants to boast must boast of what the Lord has done' Good News
7 The word used in the Good News is 'boast', and this should be used if pupils are likely to understand its meaning.

Faith
1 Good News
2 Genesis 12:1
3 Romans 4

Trusting Jesus
1 John 3:16 '…whoever believes in him shall not perish but have eternal life.'

Easter assembly

1 Genesis 1:1 NIV
2 Genesis 1:26-27
3 Genesis 3
4 Luke 19:27
5 Genesis 1:17-19
6 Romans 1:18-32
7 John 3:16
8 1 Peter 3:18 – 'For Christ died for sins once for all, the righteous for the unrighteous, to bring you to God' NIV

52 Ideas for Secondary Classroom Assemblies

Edited by Janet King with Heike Schwarz

Janet King's first bestselling book of assembly ideas is designed to help busy teachers and schools workers looking for fresh ideas and resource material for use in class-based assemblies. In many schools staff are stretched to the limit to provide relevant and effective worship. This book is a direct response to this need.

The 52 outlines draw on ideas provided by a number of experienced assembly leaders and each contains a range of ideas and activities together with suggestions for further development.

Co-published with the Association of Christian Teachers.

Monarch
Publications

ISBN 1 85424 141 9
288pp large format
Price £10.99

More Great Ideas for Secondary Classroom Assemblies

by Janet King

Contains 52 assembly outlines for busy teachers who need stimulating, practical ideas which can be used with a minimum of preparation. Each theme provides teachers with a range of ideas and activities of a broadly or specifically Christian nature.

The book recognises that schools must cater for a community in which people hold a variety of religious and non-religious commitments. The aim is to present pupils with material which encourages personal enquiry. Janet King's approach offers teachers the chance to take a fresh and exciting look at their assembly programme.

Features include:

- **Wide choice of themes**
- **Minimum of preparation required**
- **Range of activities in each outline**
- **Balanced and stimulating material**
- **Easily available resources**

Although this book is primarily designed for schools, much of the material could be adapted for use by youth groups and churches. Janet King is an independent consultant on Religious Education.

Co-published with the Association of Christian Teachers.

Monarch
Publications

ISBN 1 85424 292 X
288pp large format
Price £10.99

52 Ideas for Junior Classroom Assemblies

by Chris Chesterton and Pat Gutteridge

Assembly outlines, readings, dramas and activities for use in junior schools with individual classes and larger groups.

The book is designed to fit Key Stage Two of the National Curriculum. It is edited into three major sections: Stories from the Old Testament; Stories from the New Testament; and Life's Big Questions. The book is in a large easy-to-photocopy format and the price includes a licence to photocopy. Both authors have extensive experience of leading assemblies and training teachers.

Features include:

- **Requires minimum preparation by teacher**
- **All information needed is supplied in book**
- **Over 60 pages of material for photocopying (licence included in price)**
- **Extra strong binding**
- **Maximum pupil participation**
- **Themes directly related to children's experience**

Monarch
Publications

ISBN 1 85424 291 1
256pp large format
Price £14.99

The Good, the Bad and the Misled

by Mark Roques with Jim Tickner

'Everyone likes a good story. Mischievous teenagers will stop their banter and actually listen,' says Mark Roques. *The Good, the Bad and the Misled* is based on his years of experience as a RE teacher. An unusual feature is the inclusion of seemingly non-religious ideologies.

Each section of the book is introduced with a concise essay covering the world view concerned, and every story is followed by a series of project suggestions suitable for 14-18 year olds.

World views represented are:

- Consumerism
- Paganism
- Fascism
- Eastern religions
- Communism
- Orphism and Gnosticism
- Islam
- New Age
- Nihilism
- Primal religions
- Christianity

The price includes a licence to photocopy.

Co-published with Care for Education

Monarch
Publications

ISBN 1 85424 258 X
256pp large format
Price £9.99